Vegan Diet for Beginner

Easy 123 Recipes and 4 Weeks Diet Plan

Green Protein

2

Table of Content

Chapter One: Veganism 101

What is veganism?

Usually there is a lot of confusion over the term veganism. Most people get confused easily and more often embarrassed in public when they are asked describe what they think what vegan lifestyle entails. Many of them found difficulty in differentiating between a vegan lifestyle and a vegetarian lifestyle. To avoid this confusion and embarrassment, let's go in depth to find out exactly what veganism is.

Veganism is a philosophy, diet, and a lifestyle. Vegans survive on only products from the Plant Kingdom. They recognize the rights and value of all living creatures and follow the Golden Rule. Not only do Vegans value the life of creatures, but they also show compassion, kindness, and justice to it as well. This is one of the main reason why you don't see Vegans at zoos nor aquariums. They do not support animal exploitations in any form. For someone to follow truly follow veganism, they will have an arduous but self-fulfilling journey ahead of them.

As I have mentioned earlier, many people found difficulty differentiating between vegetarianism and veganism. The reason is that they think they are just different terms with the same meaning. That is absolutely incorrect. The words look similar to one another, but with some careful analysis, the differences is right there for the naked eye. Vegetarianism is basically a lifestyle in which people consume animal related products like milk, yogurt, butter, eggs, etc. But they refrain from consuming meat. Whereas, veganism is a lifestyle where people lack the consumption of meat and animal related products in their everyday diet; this includes milk, butter, eggs, etc. In addition, Vegans refrain themselves from ANY and

EVERY animal products. From clothing to adornments, it is hard to believe that we are surrounded by a great deal of animal related products. Fortunately, there are plenty of affordable and accessible alternatives to just about everything.

Where did veganism come from?

Vegetarianism dates back to 500 BCE from Greek philosopher and mathematician Pythagoras of Samos. He believed in benevolence of all living creatures. Around the same time, followers of Buddhism and Hinduism promoted vegetarianism with the belief that humans shouldn't inflict pain on other animals.

Fast-forward to 1847, the first vegetarian society was formed in England; three years later in 1850, Sylvester Graham, inventor of Graham Crackers, brought Vegetarianism into America when he co-founded the American Vegetarian Society. It is not until 1944 where Donald Watson created the term "Vegans" and differentiated it from vegetarians because they consumed dairy and eggs. During that year, tuberculosis was found in around 40% of dairy cows; Watson stressed on this point to convert the mass society in Veganism.

With the numerous amounts of other lifestyles in the world, why is the vegan lifestyle the right one for you? Before you choose to follow any lifestyle you must consider the gains and the losses. Vegan lifestyle isn't one to be taken half-heartedly since Veganism is an extreme form of Vegetarianism. If you have not lived at least a vegetarian lifestyle then stepping away from fast food burgers, home delivered pizza and those fried chickens will be harder than you think.

When it comes to this lifestyle you are not just stepping away from eating chicken, beef or pork. You are also stepping away from eggs which are used in such foods as bread, cake, cookies and other baked goods. You are stepping away from milk that is used in a lot of our cooking. You are stepping away from wool, leather and other products made from animal skins. As you can see the list goes on and on. It is not a case of saying that eating meats is wrong. It is a matter of saying the life of an animal is more important than what we get from them.

When living the vegan lifestyle, you have to really believe that these animals were put on the earth to live out their lives without a purpose. You need to believe that we are all here on this planet to coexist in a harmonious state where we sit around naked in front of a campfire eating the forbidden fruit.

Benefits of converting to Veganism

It is not at all surprising that the vegan lifestyle is getting so much attention throughout the world as many people are embarking on it. Many are changing their lifestyle to a vegan one for the vast benefits that it offers. This lifestyle makes you go green and support our environment too. This has a huge impact. The people around you will also be influenced by this, hence making this the best change that you can possibly do. Apart from being the best lifestyle that is there to be, it is also comparatively cheaper than the other lifestyles. Since most of the ingredients for a vegan diet can be home grown, you can save thousands of dollars on it. By avoiding eating meat, you will have no idea how much you can save every month and increase your savings and use them for other purposes.

The main nutritional consideration that you will have to make in a vegan lifestyle is to avoid chemically treated food products. It is better to use your own home grown products for your meal. Of course, you will have to go to the grocery shop once or twice in a while, but that does not mean you will have to be totally dependent on the grocery store for everything that you will need to cook a delicious meal. Almost all the ingredients for a vegan food are cheap and they are less treated with chemical products. Make sure you check this before you buy anything from the store since this can cause serious health problems.

Many people change to this diet for the health benefits it offers. People who eat meat tend to become fat easily. It is easily proven as so many people are suffering from obesity throughout the world. Hence, changing their lifestyle to a vegan one does them a load of benefit. You can easily reduce your weight in a vegan diet and you can be much healthier too. There are so many meat items that can cause serious health issues for you. Hence, one can say vegan lifestyle is the best and keeps you healthier. It is all about you curbing your instincts to eat meat and putting your head down and making the right decisions. Trust me when I say that this has all the benefits that you need from a lifestyle.

Late studies suggest that a vegan lifestyle is found to have reduced the occurrence of diabetes as well. This is something that could be debated on and conclusive proof has not yet arrived. For many people, the blood sugar levels have come down drastically after changing to a vegan lifestyle. In any case, it's better to consult your doctor for further assurances. You will definitely need your doctor's assistance if you are planning to change your lifestyle to a vegan one, as he will know condition. He will provide advice on the best course of action. This diet has also been found to reduce the use of additional medication to control the blood sugar levels in your body.

As you have decided to change your lifestyle, make sure that you have thought it through. Many people change their lifestyles without thinking and have greatly suffered. Hence, it is important to make sure that you are 100% sure of what you want. Once you have decided what you want, you should never go back. There will be minor setbacks now and then, but you will know that it is for the greater benefit. Hence, keep your head down and stay cool and just wade through the starting phase of this lifestyle. Then it will become one of the best healthy habits that you will have.

What is vegan cooking?

Separating yourself from non-consumable animal-related products is pretty simple to do due to the variety of alternatives. The difficult part is the vegan diet. Not only do you need to refrain yourself from meat, but also from products that came from a creature. This means refraining yourself from cakes, cookies, cheese, and etc since it contains dairy, eggs, and honey. Many people think that vegetables are what vegans mainly eat. However, the low calories of the content vegetables are made of does not yield enough energy for humans to use. Vegan cooking revolves more around foods such as:

Potatoes

Grains

Nuts

Leafy Greens

Legumes

The starch-rich ingredients replace meats as you are getting enough calories to get through your day.

Chapter Two: Vegan Lifestyle Guide

Tips on starting the diet

Start with alternatives

There are a variety of options you can choose from to replace the current consumption products. For example, you can replace dairy milk with the soy milk you drink daily. If you are a pizza person, there are vegan cheeses you can use and it'll still taste just as delicious.

Always snack

One of the main challenges of converting into a vegan lifestyle is due to constant hunger. If you're hungry…SNACK! Fruits such as apples, bananas, and oranges are excellent snacks filled with nutrients that will not only fill you up, but also keeps your gears running. In fact, with smoothies you can combine a variety of fruits and vegetables together and enjoy a large amount of nutrients on-the-go.

Water is key

Water will help stimulate your body in excreting toxins and wastes you have accumulated over the years of consuming animal-related products. Your body may also feel symptoms due to the changes; some of which includes headaches, frequent visits to the bathroom, and tiredness. Water will help cope with those symptoms.

Exercise

Exercising is great for all lifestyles. Studies have shown that exercising improves your attitude. So if you are struggling with this new lifestyle, EXERCISE. It doesn't have to be high intensity; going out for a walk around your neighborhood is good enough.

Surround yourself with other vegans

"Birds of the same feather flock together," not only are they similar but they are comfortable. It's never an easy journey going alone, so surround yourself with other vegans. It's easy to find people because of social media like Facebook, Twitter, or Instagram. They will be there to support you on your journey.

Shopping Guide

Shopping as a Vegan is not as hard as you think. Just keep it simple, make sure to get whole-grains, veggies, and beans. For simple and delicious dishes, I would recommend:

- Kale
- Tomatoes
- Bell peppers
- Mushroom
- Squashes
- Garlic
- Peas
- Whole grain pastas
- Rice
- Corn
- Bagels
- Sweet potatoes
- Firm Tofu

The list of ingredients goes on and on. You can also buy vinegars, olive oils, soy sauce and vegetable broth to complement with your cooking.

Guides on Eating Out

Eating out won't be as difficult as it seems if you always plan ahead. Due to the rising numbers of Vegans, there has also been an increase of vegan, if not vegetarian, restaurants. In addition, many other restaurants are also making a separate vegetarian menu due to the increasing popularity of Veganism. Even if your group of friends have a last minute change of plans, it's pretty likely you'll end up in a restaurant that will have a special vegetarian menu.

If you are unlucky and stumbled upon a restaurant that doesn't have any vegetarian menus, you can always make adjustment with the chef. For example, you can ask to take out dairy products or eggs. You can also call ahead of time and ask if the restaurant have a vegetarian menu or if they're willing to make a few adjustments. If all else fails, you can eat a bit at home and order side dishes while you're out with your friends.

Deal with cravings

If you're new to the vegan lifestyle, it's completely normal to crave the foods from your past lifestyle. The reason behind your cravings is that your body is lacking a particular nutrient. Fortunately, there are many substitutes to replaces the nutrients you're lacking.

If you are craving for chocolate, which means your body is lacking magnesium. Some substitutes would be:

- Kelp
- Oats
- Almonds & cashews
- Bananas
- Sweet potatoes
- Coffee
- Whole grains
- Brown rice

If you are craving oily foods or fatty foods like McDonalds, your body needs calcium. There are many other foods besides milk that are calcium rich. Some includes:

- Broccoli (Boiled)
- Carrots (Raw)
- Sweet potatoes (Baked)
- Soymilk
- Beans
- Firm Tofu
- Orange juice (calcium-fortified)

If you are craving meats like chicken, beef, pork, fish, etc then your body is lacking nitrogen. Nitrogen is crucial in the formation of proteins. In other words, your body isn't making as much proteins. This is a very common problem when changing into the vegan lifestyle. Substitutes includes:

- Legumes
- Cauliflower
- Asparagus

Chapter Three: Basics of Vegan Cooking

Setting up your kitchen

There are several items that are essential to set up a perfect kitchen for your vegan cuisines. Majority of them can be purchased at your local supermarket or can be home grown. Many people grow their own staple ingredients if they have a garden because of the higher nutrient values it has over store-bought item.

Store bought items:

Soy, rice, or nut milk (Great for sauces and salad dressing)

Soy sauce & tamari (Great basic sauce ingredients)

Extra-virgin olive oil

Maple syrup (Great alternative for sugar)

Agave or brown rice syrup (Excellent alternative for honey)

Cornstarch (Great thickening agent for soups)

Blender (Essential for smoothies)

Canned tomato sauce (Extremely useful for last-minute meals)

Garlic

Home grown items:

Vegetables

- Lettuces
- Peas
- Negi
- Mushrooms
- Carrots

Fruits

- Lemons
- Avocados
- Apples
- Peaches

Things to keep in mind when following the recipes

In this book, we offer a great diversity of simple yet delicious dishes. You don't have to completely follow the recipe; they were made to offer great flexibility for those who are making it. Similar to the majority of cookbooks, the prep time and cook time varies from dish to dish. So it's best for you to plan out everything if you are inviting guests over.

The portion sizes vary as well and may be different from person to person. The dishes were based upon a generic consumable amount. What is considered to be too much for you may be too little for others.

Cooking Tips

- Always wash your vegetables and fruits thoroughly before consuming them. "This avoids any consumption of dirt and minimizes chemical intake."
- Cut vegetables to bite size to be cooked faster.
- Have a volume conversion chart for reference.
- Keep your kitchen as clean as possible. "It'll impress others and a huge benefit for your health."

Chapter Four: Vegan Journey Begins

Diet plan

Just knowing the recipes is not good enough. You must have a plan of what and when to eat. Many people who are new to the vegan lifestyle will probably have trouble coming up with a diet plan. Now, I am going to suggest a simple vegan diet plan. Try it. It really works. Since you are changing your diet altogether, the first week of the new diet plan can have more calories, so that your body get used to reduce in the amount of calories and fats slowly.

The 4-week diet plan is based on less than 1200 calories a day (similar to a typical vegan diet). The amount of food from this may be inadequate, usually for men and very active individuals. If you fit into these categories, you will most likely lose weight. As I have mentioned earlier, the diet can be flexibly changed based on the person. Ask your dietitian about your normal calorie intake and modify the plan accordingly.

Note* Feel free to replace any of the recipes in this diet plan with the one that you enjoy the most from this book as long it follows the calorie count.

Week 1: The numbers in the brackets are the calories present in the food.

Monday

Breakfast: Fruity Oatmeal - 230 Calories *(Page 35)*

Lunch: Thai Peanut - 480 Calories *(Page 99)*

Dinner: Chickpea Curry - 437 Calories *(Page 150)*

Dessert: Apple Desert - 393 Calories *(Page 230)*

Tuesday

Breakfast: Marmalade - 447 Calories *(Page 72)*

Lunch: Fluffy Vegan Pancakes - 354 Calories *(Page 112)*

Dinner: Tempeh Salad - 374 Calories *(Page 184)*

Dessert: Peanut Butter Krispies - 379 Calories *(Page 224)*

Wednesday

Breakfast: Spontaneous Couscous - 356 Calories *(Page 62)*

Lunch: Raw Apple Crumble - 306 Calories *(Page 128)*

Dinner: Easy Vegan Pancakes - 424 Calories *(Page 156)*

Dessert: Chocolate Cake - 377 Calories *(Page 204)*

Thursday

Breakfast: Quinoa Tabouli - 356 Calories *(Page 42)*

Lunch: Vegan Banana Muffins - 242 Calories *(Page 134)*

Dinner: Creamy Chickpea and Tahini Casserole - 354 Calories *(Page 162)*

Dessert: Pan Fudge Cake - 369 Calories *(Page 188)*

Friday

Breakfast: Vegan Mexican Stir-Fry - 319 Calories *(Page 76)*

Lunch: Soba Noodles - 328 Calories *(Page 142)*

Dinner: Moroccan Chickpeas and Sweet Potatoes - 311 Calories *(Page 176)*

Dessert: Silky Chocolate Peanut Butter Pie - 455 Calories *(Page 196)*

Saturday

Breakfast: Spicy Chickpeas - 279 Calories *(Page 44)*

Lunch: Perfect Microwave Rice - 233 Calories *(Page 108)*

Dinner: Purple Cabbage and Pecan Salad - 241 Calories *(Page 186)*

Dessert: Thai Coconut-Mango Sticky Rice - 570 Calories *(Page 212)*

Sunday

Breakfast: Kale, Caramelized Onions & Garlic - 65 Calories *(Page 40)*

Lunch: Creamy Chickpea Curry - 752 Calories *(Page 110)*

Dinner: Spicy Hash Browns - 226 Calories *(Page 168)*

Dessert: Candied Pecans - 893 Calories *(Page 222)*

For the first week, since you are still trying to get used to a new lifestyle and totally new diet, I recommend these food items with calorific value so as to not throw off your body and keep it in balance and also you won't feel that hungry and give up in the first week itself.

Sunday's breakfast can be taken lightly as you can have more calories in the other meals of the day. I chose Sunday because, it is the only day you won't need much energy in the morning. But for people who work on Sunday too, you can change the food menu but make sure you balance it out with consuming fewer amounts of calories in your other meals. And remember, breakfast is the most important meal of the day, therefore do not skip it. Keep in mind that smoothies can be a great option for breakfast too.

Week 2: Let us start reducing the intake of calories gradually.

Monday

Breakfast: Tuscan White Bean and Spinach Soup - 218 Calories *(Page 36)*

Lunch: Mushrooms and Bell Peppers - 208 Calories *(Page 102)*

Dinner: Spinach with Pine Nuts - 180 Calories *(Page 146)*

Dessert: Pumpkin Brownie Muffins - 191 Calories *(Page 236)*

Tuesday

Breakfast: Edamame Salad - 240 Calories *(Page 46)*

Lunch: Carrot Rice with Peanuts - 199 Calories *(Page 132)*

Dinner: Indian Spiced Rice - 122 Calories *(Page 158)*

Dessert: Quick Elephant Ears - 210 Calories *(Page 240)*

Wednesday

Breakfast: Rice Salad - 210 Calories *(Page 50)*

Lunch: Garlic Quinoa - 196 Calories *(Page 126)*

Dinner: Creamy Fruit Salad - 118 Calories *(Page 164)*

Dessert: Lemon Gem Cupcakes - 225 Calories *(Page 216)*

Thursday

Breakfast: Lemon Cilantro Rice Pilaf - 204 Calories *(Page 58)*

Lunch: Vegan Bacon - 180 Calories *(Page 122)*

Dinner: Black Bean and Corn Salad - 159 Calories *(Page 174)*

Dessert: Cranberry Whip - 270 Calories *(Page 228)*

Friday

Breakfast: Wheat Flatbread - 224 Calories *(Page 68)*

Lunch: Chickpea Cutlets - 193 Calories *(Page120)*

Dinner: Parsley Salad - 165 Calories *(Page 178)*

Dessert: Fruit Salad - 279 Calories *(Page 200)*

Saturday

Breakfast: Tofu Salad - 250 Calories *(Page 78)*

Lunch: Mint Limeade - 178 Calories *(Page 118)*

Dinner: African Banana Coconut Bake - 189 Calories *(Page 180)*

Dessert: Crazy Cake - 376 Calories *(Page 242)*

Sunday

Breakfast: Kohlrabi & Carrots - 30 Calories *(Page 54)*

Lunch: Thai Style Butternut Squash Soup - 717 Calories *(Page 116)*

Dinner: Roasted Baby Red Potatoes - 117 Calories *(Page 152)*

Dessert: Baked Apple Slices - 539 Calories *(Page 234)*

I have recommended the desserts with more calories, because desserts generally tend to make you slow. So it's better to have them in weekends rather than during the weekdays when you have to work hard.

Week 3: From this week on, the calories that you are going to consume are going to go down by a great extent. The calorie levels in all the meals will be very little. So make sure you adjust whatever you want to, to get the right combination and make sure that you get enough calories required for your body to function.

Monday

Breakfast: Moroccan Vegetarian Stew - 230 Calories *(Page 86)*

Lunch: Turkish Red Lentil Soup - 188 Calories *(Page 94)*

Dinner: Tomato Basil Soup - 83 Calories *(Page 148)*

Dessert: Vegan Peanut Butter Chocolate Chip Oatmeal Cookies - 167 Calories *(Page 206)*

Tuesday

Breakfast: Spinach and Bulgar Salad - 183 Calories *(Page 82)*

Lunch: Seasoned Potatoes - 179 Calories *(Page 136)*

Dinner: Sesame Bok Choy - 75 Calories *(Page 154)*

Dessert: Peanut Butter/Corn Flakes Cookies - 160 Calories *(Page 202)*

Wednesday

Breakfast: Vegetarian Minestrone Soup - 173 Calories *(Page 80)*

Lunch: Yummy Vegan Spinach Artichoke Dip - 151 Calories *(Page 92)*

Dinner: Hummus - 73 Calories *(Page 160)*

Dessert: Zucchini Brownies - 138 Calories *(Page 198)*

Thursday

Breakfast: Spanish Green Bean Salad - 140 Calories *(Page 70)*

Lunch: Lemon Herb Quinoa - 137 Calories *(Page 106)*

Dinner: Fat Free Asian Salad Dressing - 72 Calories *(Page 172)*

Dessert: Vegan Banana Oat Cookies - 113 Calories *(Page 208)*

Friday

Breakfast: Quick and Easy Seasoned Black Beans - 166 Calories *(Page 56)*

Lunch: Sautéed Green Beans & Red Onion - 108 Calories *(Page 114)*

Dinner: Garden vegetable soup - 42 Calories *(Page 170)*

Dessert: Eggless Vegan Carrot Cake Cupcakes - 105 Calories *(Page 192)*

Saturday

Breakfast: Balsamic Tomato Couscous - 148 Calories *(Page 38)*

Lunch: Fiesta Cucumber & Corn Salad - 107 Calories *(Page 130)*

Dinner: Cheese Pasta - 99 Calories *(Page 166)*

Dessert: Scrum-Diddly-Umptious Vegan Brownies - 101 Calories *(Page 194)*

Sunday

Breakfast: Sangchu Kutjuri - 40 Calories *(Page 64)*

Lunch: Spinach-Garlic-Edamame Hummus - 641 Calories *(Page 98)*

Dinner: Kale Chips - 25 Calories *(Page 182)*

Dessert: Vegan Banana Oat Cookies - 113 Calories *(Page 208)*

Week 4: Since this is the last week, the calorie intake is meager. Let's have a look at it.

Monday

Breakfast: Vegetarian Focaccia Sandwich - 134 Calories *(Page 88)*

Lunch: Lemon Asparagus - 100 Calories *(Page 138)*

Dinner: Tomato Basil Soup - 83 Calories *(Page 148)*

Dessert: Chocolate Vegan Brownies - 120 Calories *(Page 220)*

Tuesday

Breakfast: Salsa De Cilantro – Pebre - 123 Calories *(Page 74)*

Lunch: Barking Cauliflower - 87 Calories *(Page 140)*

Dinner: Sesame Bok Choy - 75 Calories *(Page 154)*

Dessert: Healthy Banana Oatmeal Sponge Cookies - 79 Calories *(Page 214)*

Wednesday

Breakfast: Asparagus and Mushrooms - 84 Calories *(Page 84)*

Lunch: Curried Lentils - 84 Calories *(Page 96)*

Dinner: Hummus - 73 Calories *(Page 160)*

Dessert: Vegan Brownie-Oat Cookies - 78 Calories *(Page 226)*

Thursday

Breakfast: Green Beans with Lemon and Pine Nuts - 75 Calories *(Page 66)*

Lunch: Grilled Mushrooms - 64 Calories *(Page 104)*

Dinner: Fat Free Asian Salad Dressing - 72 Calories *(Page 172)*

Dessert: Cinnamon Oranges - 71 Calories *(Page 190)*

Friday

Breakfast: Oven Roasted Green Beans - 77 Calories *(Page 60)*

Lunch: Crispy Baked Radish Chips - 36 Calories *(Page 124)*

Dinner: Garden vegetable soup - 42 Calories *(Page 170)*

Dessert: Vegan Cream Cheese Frosting - 78 Calories *(Page 219)*

Saturday

Breakfast: Aubergine (Eggplant) With Raw Garlic - 71 Calories *(Page 52)*

Lunch: Za'atar Tomatoes - 92 Calories *(Page 144)*

Dinner: Cheese Pasta - 99 Calories *(Page 166)*

Dessert: Healthy Banana Oatmeal Sponge Cookies - 79 Calories *(Page 214)*

Sunday

Breakfast: Basic Black Beans - 48 Calories *(Page 48)*

Lunch: Vegan Macaroni & Cheese - 529 Calories *(Page 90)*

Dinner: Kale Chips - 25 Calories *(Page 182)*

Dessert: Chocolate Frosting - 107 Calories *(Page 232)*

I am recommending this kind of a diet plan, because after this, you will become used to every situation. You will be eating very well during the first week, and then gradually reducing the calorie levels and then almost to nothing. This way you will be prepared to whatever routine you want to follow. Once you do this, you will exactly know how much calories your body requires to function normally and choose your diet plan accordingly.

Things to keep in mind when planning your own diet?

Eating less is only half of the answer to a diet. The other half is eating right; this means you have to take in the right amount and the right nutrients if you want a healthy lifestyle. Here are some important things to keep in mind as you are planning your own vegan diet.

- A healthy vegan diet plan is around 1,200 calories

    o Keep in mind that this is not for everyone, particularly men or

      very active individuals

- Your diet plan should be included within at least 3 meals, or 3 meals

  and 2 snacks.

    o This will help sustain energy and keep hunger in check.

- Make most of your meals containing

    o Carbohydrates

    o Vegan protein

        ▪ Nuts

        ▪ beans

    o Watery, fibrous vegetables

- Broccoli

- Leafy greens

- Tomatoes

- Cucumbers

- Peppers

- You will mainly be lacking omega-3 fatty acids, protein, vitamin B-12, zinc, and calcium

  - Ask your dietitian about how to intake those lacking nutrients.

- Choose natural and whole grains food

  - They are the best at giving the most nutritional value for your calories.

  - Foods like energy bars, granola, cookies, bread, pasta often have high calories and low nutritional value.

Chapter Five: Breakfast

Fruity Oatmeal

Total cooking & preparation time: 25 Mins

Total Servings: 2

Nutritional Value (Amount Per Serving)

229.9 Calories
50 Calories from Fat
5.6 g Total Fat
0.6 g Saturated Fat
0 mg Cholesterol
5.8 mg Sodium
43.8 g Total Carbohydrate
5.7 g Dietary Fiber
23.2 g Sugars
4.6 g Protein

Ingredients

- 1⁄2 cup oatmeal
- 1⁄2 cup apple juice, frozen
- 1⁄2 cup water
- 1 apple, small & diced
- 3 prunes, diced
- 3 apricots, dehydrated, dried & diced
- 4 pecans, diced
- 1⁄4 tsp. cinnamon

Cooking Directions

1. In a sauce pan, preferably small; mix together the frozen apple juice and water, bring to a boil.

2. Add in half cup of oatmeal, approximately a minute. The moment it's cooked as per the directions mentioned on the box, remove it from the heat and let it stand for couple of minutes to cool a little and thicken.

3. Add in the pecans, cinnamon and the fruit pieces; as you're adding in, don't forget to stir and don't let them stick together.

4. To preserve more of vitamins, wait till the oatmeal is cool and then add in the fruits.

Tuscan White Bean and Spinach Soup

Total cooking & preparation time: 25 Mins

Total Servings: 4

Nutritional Value (Amount Per Serving)

218.4 Calories
30 Calories from Fat
3.3 g Total Fat
0.5 g Saturated Fat
0 mg Cholesterol
726.3 mg Sodium
37.9 g Total Carbohydrate
7.8 g Dietary Fiber
3.4 g Sugars
12 g Protein

Ingredients

- 3 cups Baby Spinach, cleaned & trimmed
- 1 can white beans, cannellini (approximately 14 1/2 oz.)
- 1 finely diced shallot
- 3 to 4 cups vegetable stock
- 1 finely minced garlic clove
- 1 can tomatoes, diced (approximately 14 1/2 oz.)
- 1 tsp. rosemary
- 1/2 cup shell pasta or 1/2 cup pasta shells, whole wheat
- 2 tsp. olive oil

- 1 dash red pepper flakes, crushed
- 1/8 tsp. black pepper

Cooking Directions

1. Heat olive oil in a sauce pan, preferably large & sauté the garlic & shallots.

2. Add tomatoes, broth, rosemary and beans to the pot. Season it with red and black pepper and bring to a boil.

3. Put the pasta in & cook approximately 10 mins. Add a small quantity of broth more, if the soup seems too thick.

4. Add spinach & cook until heated through and wilted.

Balsamic Tomato Couscous

Total cooking & preparation time: 20 Mins

Total Servings: 8

Nutritional Value (Amount Per Serving)

148.3 Calories
13 Calories from Fat
1.4 g Total Fat
0.2 g Saturated Fat
0 mg Cholesterol
7.6 mg Sodium
28.6 g Total Carbohydrate
2.4 g Dietary Fiber
2.4 g Sugars
4.7 g Protein

Ingredients

- 5 tomatoes, small
- 2 cups vegetable broth, nonfat
- 3 tbsp. balsamic vinegar
- 1 1/2 cups couscous, uncooked
- 1 tsp. basil, dried
- 1 tsp. garlic, minced
- 2 tsp. olive oil
- 1/4 tsp. pepper, ground

Cooking Directions

1. Bring the broth to a boil in a pan, preferably medium size.

2. Add the garlic and basil, when it's boiling, stirring frequently. Add the couscous to the pan, cover & remove let it heat, approximately 5 to 10 minutes.

3. Chop the tomatoes.

4. Mix together the balsamic vinegar, pepper, and the oil in a small bowl and then add the tomatoes.

5. Add the tomato mixture, when the couscous is ready & mix well.

6. Serve cold or hot.

Kale, Caramelized Onions & Garlic

Total cooking & preparation time: 22 Mins

Total Servings: 4

Nutritional Value (Amount Per Serving)

65.3 Calories
33 Calories from Fat
3.8 g Total Fat
0.5 g Saturated Fat
0 mg Cholesterol
22.8 mg Sodium
7.4 g Total Carbohydrate
1.4 g Dietary Fiber
0.8 g Sugars
2 g Protein

Ingredients

- 3 garlic cloves, chopped
- 1 bunch kale, washed & torn (stems removed)
- balsamic vinegar
- 1 onion, small & chopped
- 1 tbsp. olive oil

Cooking Directions

1. In a large pan, heat the olive oil.

2. Add chopped garlic and onions.

3. Sauté onions until begin to caramelize and are clear, stirring often. Keep an eye on the garlic as well. Don't allow it to burn.

4. Add the torn kale and toss with garlic and onions. Cook until kale is wilted.

5. If desired, drizzle small quantity of balsamic vinegar.

Quinoa Tabouli

Total cooking & preparation time: 25 Mins

Total Servings: 1

Nutritional Value (Amount Per Serving)

356 Calories
189 Calories from Fat
21.1 g Total Fat
2.9 g Saturated Fat
0 mg Cholesterol
28.4 mg Sodium
36.5 g Total Carbohydrate
5.8 g Dietary Fiber
4 g Sugars
8.1 g Protein

Ingredients

- 3 ripe tomatoes, medium
- 1 cup scallion, chopped
- 1 cup quinoa
- 2 cups water
- 1/2 cup lemon juice, fresh
- 2 tbsp. mint, fresh
- 1.5 cups coarsely chopped parsley
- salt to taste
- 1/3 cup olive oil

Cooking Directions

1. In a colander, arrange the quinoa & rinse a lot of times, to get rid of the sour outer layer, rub the grains together.

2. Place quinoa & water into a saucepan, preferably 2-quart and bring to boil. Decrease the heat settings and allow it to simmer. Cover & cook until quinoa absorbs almost all water, approximately 10 - 15 minutes.

3. Chop the parsley, scallions, and tomatoes finely while quinoa is still cooking. Add fresh mint, olive oil & lemon juice to tomato mixture.

4. Stir in salt and cooked quinoa. Mix well.

5. To blend the flavors completely, let the tabouli to sit in a refrigerator approximately a day.

6. Remove the Tabouli from the refrigerator almost an hour before serving as it's served traditionally at the room temperature.

Spicy Chickpeas

Total cooking & preparation time: 25 Mins

Total Servings: 5

Nutritional Value (Amount Per Serving)

Calories 271.2
Calories from Fat 68
Total Fat 7.6 g
Saturated Fat 0.9 g
Cholesterol 0 mg
Sodium 749.7 mg
Total Carbohydrate 43 g
Dietary Fiber 8.6 g
Sugars 2.3 g
Protein 9.2 g

Ingredients

- 2 cans garbanzo beans, drained (approximately 15 oz.)
- 1 onion, chopped
- 1 tsp. cumin seed
- 2 tomatoes, chopped
- 1/2 tsp. lemon pepper
- 1 tbsp. lemon juice
- 2 tbsp. vegetable oil
- 1/2 tsp. chili powder
- 1/2 tsp. salt

Cooking Directions

1. Warm oil & cumin over low heat in a large pot; heat cumin until it turns a darker brown shade.

2. Add pepper seasoning, lemon, chili powder and salt; mix well.

3. Stir in the tomatoes; add in the chickpeas, once the juice begins to thicken and mix well.

4. Add in the lemon juice & mix well; add onions and stir until onions become soft.

5. Remove the pot from the heat & place into a serving bowl.

6. Serve hot.

Edamame Salad

Total cooking & preparation time: 20 Mins

Total Servings: 8

Nutritional Value (Amount Per Serving)

240.4 Calories
76 Calories from Fat
8.5 g Total Fat
1.1 g Saturated Fat
0 mg Cholesterol
276.6 mg Sodium
35.9 g Total Carbohydrate
6.5 g Dietary Fiber
1.6 g Sugars
11.8 g Protein

Ingredients

- 3 cups petite corn kernels, frozen
- 1 pound shelled edamame, frozen
- 1 red bell pepper, chopped
- 1/4 cup Italian parsley, fresh & chopped
- 1/2 cup red onion, finely chopped
- 3/4 cup sliced onion, green
- 2 tbsp. oregano, fresh & chopped or 2 tbsp. basil or 2 tbsp. marjoram

For Dressing

- 2 tbsp. Dijon mustard
- 1/3 cup fresh lemon juice
- 2 tbsp. olive oil
- 3/4 tsp. black pepper, fresh & ground
- 3/4 tsp. salt

Cooking Directions

1. Prepare the edamame as per the directions mentioned on the package. Drain & rinse using cold water. Keep it aside to drain thoroughly.

2. Mix together the corn, edamame, green onion, red bell pepper, oregano, red onion, and parsley.

3. Whisk olive oil, lemon juice, mustard, pepper and salt together in a large bowl. Add the veggies to the bowl & toss to evenly coat. Refrigerate the final mixture until ready to serve.

Basic Black Beans

Total cooking & preparation time: 20 Mins

Total Servings: 6

Nutritional Value (Amount Per Serving)

48.7 Calories
23 Calories from Fat
2.7 g Total Fat
0.4 g Saturated Fat
0 mg Cholesterol
199.6 mg Sodium
6.1 g Total Carbohydrate
1.5 g Dietary Fiber
2.6 g Sugars
1.2 g Protein

Ingredients

- 2 cups tomatoes, fresh, skinned & chopped or 2 cans tomatoes, diced & drained
- 4 cups black beans, cooked or 4 cans black beans, drained & rinsed
- 2 tbsp. garlic, minced
- 2 onions, small & chopped
- 1/4 tsp. cayenne pepper
- 2 tsp. cumin, ground
- 1/2 tsp. oregano
- 1 1/2 tsp. coriander, ground
- 1 tbsp. olive oil
- 1/4 tsp. black pepper
- 1/2 tsp. salt

Cooking Directions

1. Over medium high heat settings in large skillet, heat the olive oil and sauté garlic, onions & spices until onions are soft.

2. Add tomatoes & beans, cook until bubbly.

3. Decrease the heat settings to low. Cover; cook approximately 10 minutes.

4. If required, add salt.

5. Serve over cornbread or hot cooked rice.

Rice Salad

Total cooking & preparation time: 30 Mins

Total Servings: 8

Nutritional Value (Amount Per Serving)

210.9 Calories
91 Calories from Fat
10.1 g Total Fat
1.2 g Saturated Fat
0 mg Cholesterol
159.4 mg Sodium
26.6 g Total Carbohydrate
2.2 g Dietary Fiber
2.5 g Sugars
4.1 g Protein

Ingredients

- 1 cup rice
- 1/2 cup onion, chopped
- 1 cup celery, chopped
- 1/2 cup corn, canned
- 1/2 cup peas, canned

For Dressing

- 1/3 cup almonds, chopped
- 1 tsp. vinegar
- 1 tsp. curry powder

- 1 tbsp. soy sauce
- 1 tsp. sugar
- 1⁄4 cup oil

Cooking Directions

1. Put slightly salted water in a saucepan and cook 1 cup of rice. Let it cool at room temperature.

2. Add the vegetables to the rice & mix well.

3. Add all of the dressing ingredients to the mixture. Mix again and refrigerate for a minimum period of an hour.

4. Add almonds, just before serving.

Aubergine (Eggplant) With Raw Garlic

Total cooking & preparation time: 20 Mins

Total Servings: 4

Nutritional Value (Amount Per Serving)

71.5 Calories
33 Calories from Fat
3.7 g Total Fat
0.5 g Saturated Fat
0 mg Cholesterol
589 mg Sodium
9.8 g Total Carbohydrate
5 g Dietary Fiber
3.5 g Sugars
1.8 g Protein

Ingredients

- 1 eggplant, large
- 2 tbsp. lemon juice, fresh
- olive oil, extra-virgin, as needed
- 1 tbsp. olive oil, extra virgin
- 4 garlic cloves, peeled & finely minced
- 1/2 cup flat leaf parsley, fresh & finely chopped
- 1 tsp. salt

Cooking Directions

1. Wash the eggplant well using cold water and then cut off the stem portion (Don't peel them).

2. Slice the eggplant into slices, preferably ¼" & brush olive oil, preferably extra virgin on each side.

3. Over medium-high heat settings in a nonstick skillet, brown the eggplant slices until golden brown on each side.

4. Arrange the cooked eggplant slices on a serving platter.

5. Mix together lemon juice, garlic, salt & one tbsp olive oil in a small measuring cup.

6. Drizzle this mixture over the eggplant slices and sprinkle parsley at the top. Serve immediately.

Kohlrabi & Carrots

Total cooking & preparation time: 25 Mins

Total Servings: 4

Nutritional Value (Amount Per Serving)

30.3 Calories
2 Calories from Fat
0.2 g Total Fat
0.1 g Saturated Fat
0 mg Cholesterol
49.7 mg Sodium
7 g Total Carbohydrate
2 g Dietary Fiber
3.4 g Sugars
0.7 g Protein

Ingredients

- 1 kohlrabi, medium, peeled & chopped into cubes, preferably ¾" (approximately 2 cups)
- 4 carrots, large & cut into chunks (matching the size of kohlrabi)
- 1 tbsp. butter (optional)
- 1/4 tsp. nutmeg
- pepper and salt, to taste

Cooking Directions

1. Boil the carrots and Kohlrabi in water, lightly salted approximately 15 to 20 minutes, until quite tender. Drain it well.

2. Mash lightly, leaving a lot of texture. Don't mash them completely and look like mashed potatoes.

3. Add butter and nutmeg.

4. Serve.

Quick and Easy Seasoned Black Beans

Total cooking & preparation time: 30 Mins

Total Servings: 6

Nutritional Value (Amount Per Serving)

166.2 Calories
20 Calories from Fat
2.3 g Total Fat
0.4 g Saturated Fat
0 mg Cholesterol
4.4 mg Sodium
28.2 g Total Carbohydrate
9.7 g Dietary Fiber
1.1 g Sugars
9.7 g Protein

Ingredients

- 2 cans black beans, (approximately 15 oz.)
- 1 onion, medium & finely chopped
- 2 jalapeno chiles, finely chopped (if desired, you may remove the seeds)
- 1 tsp. Mexican oregano
- 2 tsp. cumin, ground
- 2 tbsp. lime juice, fresh
- 1/2 cup cilantro, fresh & chopped
- 2 tbsp. garlic, chopped
- 2 tsp. olive oil, extra virgin
- Black pepper and salt (to taste)

Cooking Directions

1. Heat oil over medium heat settings in a large saucepan & sauté the garlic.

2. As oil begins to warm, add jalapeño and onion.

3. Add cumin and oregano and sauté until vegetables are almost tender (if they begin to stick, you may add some drops of water), stirring frequently.

4. Add canned black beans & bring to a boil.

5. Decrease the heat settings & to let the flavors to blend, simmer approximately half an hour.

6. Add lime juice and chopped cilantro and stir.

7. Serve

Lemon Cilantro Rice Pilaf

Total cooking & preparation time: 30 Mins

Total Servings: 4

Nutritional Value (Amount Per Serving)

204.3 Calories
33 Calories from Fat
3.8 g Total Fat
0.5 g Saturated Fat
0 mg Cholesterol
152.4 mg Sodium
38.3 g Total Carbohydrate
1.1 g Dietary Fiber
0.4 g Sugars
3.5 g Protein

Ingredients

- 1 cup raw rice, long grain
- 1 tbsp. lemon rind, fresh & grated
- 1/2 tsp. turmeric, ground
- 1 tbsp. lemon juice
- 1/4 cup cilantro, fresh & chopped
- 1/3 cup green onion, sliced
- 1 1/2 cups water
- 1 tbsp. oil
- 1/4 tsp. salt

Cooking Directions

1. In nonstick sauce pan heat oil over medium high heat settings.

2. Add rice & sauté until the rice kernels becomes opaque.

3. Add grated lemon rind, water, lemon juice, salt and turmeric.

4. Cover; decrease the heat settings & simmer approximately 15 minutes.

5. Stir in cilantro and green onions

Oven Roasted Green Beans

Total cooking & preparation time: 20 Mins

Total Servings: 4

Nutritional Value (Amount Per Serving)

77 Calories
37 Calories from Fat
4.2 g Total Fat
0.5 g Saturated Fat
0 mg Cholesterol
7.2 mg Sodium
9.3 g Total Carbohydrate
3.6 g Dietary Fiber
4 g Sugars
2.9 g Protein

Ingredients

- 1 -1 1/4 pound yellow wax bean, trimmed or 1 -1 1/4 pound green beans (can even use a mixture of both)
- 1/2 tsp. basil, dried
- 2 tbsp. almonds, slivered
- 1 tsp. lemon zest
- 1 tbsp. lemon juice
- 1/2 tsp. garlic powder
- 2 to 4 tsp. olive oil
- Black pepper, freshly ground & salt to taste

Cooking Directions

1. Preheat your oven to 450 F/225 C.

2. Line a roasting or baking pan with foil & spray with non stick spray.

3. Mix all the ingredients together on the pan and using your hands, toss well (make sure that all the beans are coated evenly).

4. Bake in the oven until the beans are slightly browned and tender, approximately 10 minutes.

5. While the beans are cooking, you may still toss them a couple of times.

Spontaneous Couscous

Total cooking & preparation time: 25 Mins

Total Servings: 1

Nutritional Value (Amount Per Serving)

356.3 Calories
52 Calories from Fat
5.8 g Total Fat
0.9 g Saturated Fat
0 mg Cholesterol
51 mg Sodium
69.2 g Total Carbohydrate
7.8 g Dietary Fiber
8.5 g Sugars
10.6 g Protein

Ingredients

- 1 chopped cup onion
- 1 minced garlic clove
- 1/2 cup corn, frozen
- 1/4 cup couscous
- 1/2 tomatoes, medium & chopped
- 1 tsp. Tabasco sauce
- 1 tsp. chopped parsley
- 1/8 tsp. cayenne
- 1 tsp. olive oil
- 1/2 cup water
- Pepper and salt to taste

Cooking Directions

1. Heat oil over medium low heat settings in a pan, and then sauté the onions and garlic until onions are slightly browned approximately 10 minutes, stirring occasionally.

2. Add water, corn, couscous and tomatoes.

3. Cover; cook on low heat until the couscous is soft and the water is completely absorbed, approximately for 5 to 10 minutes.

4. Add Tabasco, cayenne and parsley.

5. Pepper and salt to taste, if desired.

Sangchu Kutjuri

Total cooking & preparation time: 20 Mins

Total Servings: 4

Nutritional Value (Amount Per Serving)

40.8 Calories
22 Calories from Fat
2.4 g Total Fat
0.3 g Saturated Fat
0 mg Cholesterol
272.9 mg Sodium
3.3 g Total Carbohydrate
1.1 g Dietary Fiber
1 g Sugars
1.7 g Protein

Ingredients

- 2 scallions, large & chopped
- 1 head red leaf lettuce, torn
- 1 tbsp. soy sauce
- 1/2 tsp. red pepper flakes, crushed
- 2 tsp. cider vinegar
- 1/4 tsp. sugar
- 2 tsp. sesame oil

Cooking Directions

1. Arrange the lettuce in a salad bowl, preferably large.

2. In mixing bowl, preferably medium size, mix together the scallions, sesame oil soy sauce, sugar, cider vinegar, & red pepper flakes, stirring well.

3. Transfer the mixture over the lettuce, toss well & serve immediately

Green Beans with Lemon and Pine Nuts

Total cooking & preparation time: 25 Mins

Total Servings: 8

Nutritional Value (Amount Per Serving)

75.2 Calories
47 Calories from Fat
5.3 g Total Fat
0.6 g Saturated Fat
0 mg Cholesterol
5.8 mg Sodium
6.6 g Total Carbohydrate
2.5 g Dietary Fiber
3 g Sugars
2.2 g Protein

Ingredients

- 1⁄4 cup pine nuts, toasted
- 1 1⁄2 pounds green beans, trimmed & cut into ½" pieces, diagonally
- 1 1⁄2 tsp. lemon zest, fresh & finely grated
- 4 tsp. olive oil, extra virgin
- 2 tbsp. flat-leaf parsley, fresh & finely chopped
- Pepper & salt to taste

Cooking Directions

1. In a saucepan, preferably 4-quart, add boiling salted water & cook the beans approximately 5 minutes, until just tender. Using a colander, drain the beans well.

2. Transfer the beans to a salad bowl & toss with oil, parsley, nuts, and zest. Season with pepper and salt to taste.

Wheat Flatbread

Total cooking & preparation time: 20 Mins

Total Servings: 6

Nutritional Value (Amount Per Serving)

224 Calories
87 Calories from Fat
9.8 g Total Fat
1.3 g Saturated Fat
0 mg Cholesterol
389.2 mg Sodium
30.3 g Total Carbohydrate
2.7 g Dietary Fiber
0.1 g Sugars
4.8 g Protein

Ingredients

- 1 cup flour, all-purpose
- 1 cup flour, whole wheat
- 4 tbsp. vegetable oil
- 2/3 cup warm water
- 1 tsp. salt

Cooking Directions

1. Mix together the flours.

2. Dissolve salt into water and then add water & oil to the flour, mixing well.

3. Briefly knead on the floured surface and allow it to rest approximately 10 to 15 minutes.

4. Cut into equal parts, preferably 12.

5. Don't stack the parts, just roll each part flat.

6. Cook on griddle, ungreased until golden brown, a few minutes on each side.

7. After removing from the griddle, brush with olive oil or melted butter immediately.

Spanish Green Bean Salad

Total cooking & preparation time: 20 Mins

Total Servings: 6

Nutritional Value (Amount Per Serving)

140 Calories
84 Calories from Fat
9.4 g Total Fat
1.3 g Saturated Fat
0 mg Cholesterol
108.8 mg Sodium
13.7 g Total Carbohydrate
4.4 g Dietary Fiber
7.2 g Sugars
3 g Protein

Ingredients

- 2 oz. red bell peppers, roasted, skinned & diced
- 1 to 2 tsp. sugar
- 2 pounds green beans, ends trimmed & cut into pieces, preferably 1"
- 1/2 red onion, small & minced
- 2 tbsp. balsamic vinegar (may also use white vinegar)
- 1/8 tsp. pepper
- 2 tbsp. lemon juice
- lettuce, shredded to serve
- 2 tbsp. parsley, fresh & chopped finely
- 1/4 cup olive oil
- 1/4 to 1/2 tsp. salt

Cooking Directions

1. Use a small amount of boiling water to cook the beans in a pan. Or you can cook in a microwave until tender but still crisp, approximately 6 to 7 minutes.

2. Put olive oil, red bell peppers, balsamic vinegar, red onion, lemon juice, sugar, parsley, pepper & salt in a jar with a lid. Cover; shaking well.

3. Put the dressing mixture over the beans, stirring well & put them in a refrigerator.

4. Remove the beans from the refrigerator an hour before serving and serve over shredded lettuce.

Absolutely Fail-Proof Easy Marmalade

Total cooking & preparation time: 30 Mins

Total Servings: 5

Nutritional Value (Amount Per Serving)

847.9 Calories
1 Calories from Fat
0.2 g Total Fat
0 g Saturated Fat
0 mg Cholesterol
2 mg Sodium
218.4 g Total Carbohydrate
3.8 g Dietary Fiber
214.3 g Sugars
1.5 g Protein

Ingredients

* 1 kg sugar
* 6 grapefruits or 6 oranges or 6 lemons

Cooking Directions

1. Wash the citrus fruits well using cold water, remove any blemishes.

2. Cut the fruits into quarters & place them in a food processor.

3. Chop finely the ground, skin & all.

4. Add a small quantity of crystallized ginger, if you want.

5. Using a wooden spoon, boil with sugar, approximately 20 minutes, stirring occasionally.

6. Be careful as it may splatter.

7. This quantity would fill the jars, approximately 5 x 340 gram.

8. You may refrigerate it up to 6 months without changing the bottles.

Salsa De Cilantro – Pebre

Total cooking & preparation time: 20 Mins

Total Servings: 3

Nutritional Value (Amount Per Serving)

123.6 Calories
85 Calories from Fat
9.5 g Total Fat
1.2 g Saturated Fat
0 mg Cholesterol
259.3 mg Sodium
9.4 g Total Carbohydrate
2.4 g Dietary Fiber
5.3 g Sugars
1.9 g Protein

Ingredients

- 4 tomatoes, medium & chopped
- 1 tbsp. white vinegar
- 1/3 cup scallions or onion, minced
- 2 tbsp. Tabasco hot sauce
- 1/2 cup cilantro, fresh & finely chopped
- 2 tbsp. vegetable oil
- 2 garlic cloves, minced or pressed
- 1 tbsp. lime juice, fresh
- Pepper & salt to taste

Cooking Directions

1. In a bowl, preferably medium size, mix everything together & refrigerate for 3 to 4 days.

Vegan Mexican Stir-Fry

Total cooking & preparation time: 20 Mins

Total Servings: 2

Nutritional Value (Amount Per Serving)

318.9 Calories
18 Calories from Fat
2.1 g Total Fat
0.4 g Saturated Fat
0 mg Cholesterol
115 mg Sodium
66 g Total Carbohydrate
12.8 g Dietary Fiber
2.9 g Sugars
13.2 g Protein

Ingredients

- 1 cup black beans, cooked
- 1/2 onion, small & diced
- 1 cup brown rice, cooked
- 1/2 diced green pepper
- 1 tbsp. taco seasoning
- 1/2 cup tomato, canned & diced
- 1/2 cup corn, frozen
- hot sauce
- salt

Cooking Directions

1. Use cooking spray to spray a non-stick skillet and over medium heat, sauté onion and green pepper just a few minutes, until onion is translucent.

2. Add the remaining ingredients & cook approximately 3 to 5 minutes. Just spoon into a bowl & top with Jalapenos, avocado, cheese, olives, etc.

3. You may use two small Tupperware to store the remaining tomatoes, frozen for later use.

Tofu Salad

Total cooking & preparation time: 15 Mins

Total Servings: 4

Nutritional Value (Amount Per Serving)

249.5 Calories
59 Calories from Fat
6.7 g Total Fat
1.1 g Saturated Fat
7.2 mg Cholesterol
473.2 mg Sodium
41.3 g Total Carbohydrate
2.1 g Dietary Fiber
4.1 g Sugars
6 g Protein

Ingredients

- 1 tsp. basil
- 1/4 cup of each green & red pepper
- 1 package tofu (extra firm or firm)
- 1/2 cup onion, diced
- 1 tsp. cumin
- 1/2 cup mayonnaise, vegan
- 1 tsp. parsley
- 4 pita pockets

Cooking Directions

1. Cut the tofu into half inch cubes & fry until golden brown, for few minutes. Mix tofu with onions, mayo, seasonings (any of your choice) and peppers.

2. Depending on your liking, you may add more or less quantity mayo to the salad.

3. Use a pita pocket to serve.

Vegetarian Minestrone Soup

Total cooking & preparation time: 55 Mins

Total Servings: 6

Nutritional Value (Amount Per Serving)

172.4 Calories
39 Calories from Fat
4.4 g Total Fat
0.7 g Saturated Fat
0 mg Cholesterol
577.8 mg Sodium
28.6 g Total Carbohydrate
7 g Dietary Fiber
9.2 g Sugars
6.6 g Protein

Ingredients

- 28 oz. fluid canned plum tomatoes, dice & include liquid
- 1⁄4 cup elbow macaroni or 1⁄4 cup uncooked ditalini
- 2 cups zucchini, diced
- 1 tsp. basil, dried or 2 tbsp. basil, fresh & finely chopped
- 3⁄4 cup onion, chopped
- 1 cup cannellini beans, canned or 1 cup white beans
- 3⁄4 cup celery, diced
- 1 cup carrot, peeled & diced
- 1⁄8 tsp. black pepper, fresh & coarse ground
- 2 minced garlic cloves
- 1 tbsp. olive oil, extra virgin
- 3 cups water

- 1/4 tsp. oregano, dried
- 1/4 tsp. salt

Cooking Directions

1. Over medium-high heat in a large saucepan, heat the oil.

2. Add chopped onion to the pan & sauté until just lightly browned, approximately 4 minutes.

3. Add water, carrots, zucchini, celery, cannellini beans, basil, pepper, oregano salt, garlic and tomatoes.

4. Bring the mixture to a boil; decrease the heat settings, cover; simmer on medium-low heat approximately half an hour, stirring rarely.

5. Put the macaroni in the mixture. Cover; cook approximately 10 more minutes.

6. Adjust the spices to your likings.

7. Serve hot.

Spinach and Bulgar Salad

Total cooking & preparation time: 20 Mins

Total Servings: 4

Nutritional Value (Amount Per Serving)

183.2 Calories
121 Calories from Fat
13.5 g Total Fat
5.5 g Saturated Fat
26.8 mg Cholesterol
385.4 mg Sodium
9.6 g Total Carbohydrate
2.8 g Dietary Fiber
1.7 g Sugars
7 g Protein

Ingredients

- 4 oz. feta cheese, crumbled
- 1/3 cup thinly sliced onion, green
- 1/4 cup red wine vinegar
- 1/2-pound spinach leaves, rinsed & drained
- 1/3 cup dill, fresh & chopped
- 2 tbsp. olive oil
- 1 cup cherry tomatoes, cut in half
- Pepper and salt

Cooking Directions

1. Combine one and half cups of boiling water and bulgur in a bowl, preferably small size. Let the bulgur to stand approximately 15 minutes, until it's tender to bite.

2. In the meantime, stack the spinach leaves & cut into strips, ¼" wide.

3. In a wide bowl, place the onions, spinach, cheese, and dill. Remove the excess water from the bulgur by transferring it to a fine strainer & pressing. Now add the bulgur to the bowl with spinach.

4. Mix oil and vinegar. Add the oil mixture to the salad & mix well. Season with pepper and salt to taste.

Asparagus and Mushrooms

Total cooking & preparation time: 20 Mins

Total Servings: 4

Nutritional Value (Amount Per Serving)

84.9 Calories
35 Calories from Fat
4 g Total Fat
0.6 g Saturated Fat
0 mg Cholesterol
191.1 mg Sodium
10.2 g Total Carbohydrate
3.8 g Dietary Fiber
4 g Sugars
5.5 g Protein

Ingredients

- 4 green onions, sliced in pieces, preferably ½"
- 1 pound asparagus, trimmed
- 2 tsp. soy sauce
- 2 tomatoes, small & each cut into 8 wedges
- 1 tsp. cornstarch
- 1/2 pound sliced mushroom,
- 1 tbsp. cold water
- 1 tbsp. oil

Cooking Directions

1. Cut the asparagus into pieces, preferably 1".

2. Sauté green onion and asparagus in oil approximately 4 minutes.

3. Put the mushrooms in the mixture & cook for a minute more.

4. Mix soy sauce, corn starch and water.

5. Stir into the asparagus until thick. Add tomatoes & toss well.

Moroccan vegetarian stew

Total cooking & preparation time: 45 Mins

Total Servings: 6

Nutritional Value (Amount Per Serving)

229.2 Calories
12 Calories from Fat
1.4 g Total Fat
0.2 g Saturated Fat
0 mg Cholesterol
459.5 mg Sodium
51.4 g Total Carbohydrate
8.5 g Dietary Fiber
13.5 g Sugars
6.5 g Protein

Ingredients

- 2 sweet potatoes, cut into cubes, preferably 1"
- 1 can chickpeas, rinsed & drained (15 ounce)
- 1 tsp. turmeric
- 1/2 tsp. curry powder
- 1 Spanish onion, large & diced
- 1/2 tsp. cumin
- 3 carrots, cut into rounds, preferably 1"
- 1/4 tsp. red pepper flakes
- 2 minced garlic cloves
- 3/4 tsp. cinnamon
- 1 can whole tomatoes (15 ounce)
- 1/4 tsp. ground nutmeg

- 1 acorn squash, cut into cubes, preferably 1"
- 1⁄2 cup vegetable broth
- 1⁄2 cup raisins
- 1⁄2 tsp. pepper
- 1⁄2 tsp. salt

Cooking Directions

1. Over low heat settings in a pot, sauté garlic and onions until soft, don't make them brown.

2. Add spices & cook for a few minutes. Stir in broth, sweet potatoes, acorn squash and carrots and bring this mixture to a boil.

3. Decrease the heat settings to low & simmer approximately 5 minutes, covered.

4. Add raisins, chick peas and tomatoes, simmer until the carrots, squash and potatoes are tender, approximately half an hour, covered.

Vegetarian Focaccia Sandwich

Total cooking & preparation time: 15 Mins

Total Servings: 8

Nutritional Value (Amount Per Serving)

134 Calories
95 Calories from Fat
10.6 g Total Fat
5 g Saturated Fat
22.4 mg Cholesterol
136 mg Sodium
4.3 g Total Carbohydrate
1.2 g Dietary Fiber
2.2 g Sugars
6.3 g Protein

Ingredients

- 6 oz. cheddar cheese, shredded
- 1 onion, medium
- 6 oz. portabella mushrooms
- 2 large peppers (orange, green, yellow or red, of your choice)
- 1/4 cup mustard, dijon-style
- 16 oz. loaf focaccia bread
- 2 tbsp. olive oil

Cooking Directions

1. Slice the bread lengthwise in half.

2. Slice the peppers into slices, preferably 1/8".

3. Slice mushrooms and onion.

4. Over medium heat in a skillet, heat the oil.

5. Add onions and peppers, and continue to cook until onions begin to soften.

6. Add mushrooms & cook until soft.

7. Spread the mustard mixture & sprinkle with cheese on each half of bread

8. On the top of half bread with the mushroom mixture, place the other half of the bread.

9. Cut and make 8 slices out of it

Chapter Six: Lunch

Vegan Macaroni & Cheese

Total cooking and preparation time: 35 minutes

Servings:4

Nutritional Value (Amount Per Serving)

529 Calories
147 Calories from Fat
16.4 g Total Fat
3 g Saturated Fat
0 mg Cholesterol
509.4 mg Sodium
75.3 g Total Carbohydrate
9.6 g Dietary Fiber
6.5 g Sugars
23.4 g Protein

Ingredients

- 8 oz. elbow macaroni, cooked & drained
- 1/2 tsp. mustard powder or 1/2 tsp. mustard, prepared
- 1/2 cup wheat flour or 1/2 cup white flour
- 1/4 tsp. paprika
- 1/2 cup nutritional yeast flakes
- 2 cups soymilk
- 2 to 3 chopped cloves garlic or 1 to 2 tsp. garlic powder
- 1/4 cup oil or 1/4 cup margarine
- 1/2 to 1 tsp. salt

Cooking Directions

1. In a saucepan, mix together all of the dry ingredients and then whisk in the milk.

2. Cook over medium heat settings until it thickens & begin to bubble, whisking constantly.

3. Cook & stir approximately half a minute more and then remove it from the heat.

4. Whip in the mustard & margarine.

5. If the mixture is too thick, add more water or milk.

6. Add macaroni, hot & cooked; mix well.

7. Serve hot & enjoy!

Yummy Vegan Spinach Artichoke Dip

Total cooking and preparation time: 30 minutes

Servings: 6

Nutritional Value (Amount Per Serving)

151.9 Calories
49 Calories from Fat
5.5 g Total Fat
0.8 g Saturated Fat
0 mg Cholesterol
482.5 mg Sodium
16.6 g Total Carbohydrate
9.6 g Dietary Fiber
1.9 g Sugars
13.8 g Protein

Ingredients:

- 1 package tofu, firm & silken (12 oz.)
- 1 package spinach, frozen, chopped, thawed, drained & squeezed dry (approximately 12 oz)
- 3 garlic cloves
- 2 to 3 tbsp. apple cider vinegar
- 1/2 cup nutritional yeast flakes
- 1 jar artichoke hearts, marinated (8 oz)
- 1 tsp. parsley, dried
- 1/2 onion, yellow & diced
- 1 tsp. basil, dried
- 1/4 tsp. cayenne pepper
- 1 tbsp. olive oil

- 1/2 tsp. black pepper
- 1 tsp. salt

Cooking Directions:

1. Preheat your oven to 175 C/350 F.

2. Sauté the artichoke hearts, spinach and onion in olive oil approximately 6 minutes, until onion is soft.

3. Blend nutritional yeast, tofu, spices, vinegar & garlic together in a blender until smooth and mixed well.

4. Mix all the ingredients together.

5. Taste and if required, you may add additional quantity of nutritional yeast and seasonings.

6. Smooth into a baking dish, preferably non-stick & bake until lightly browned on the top, approximately 15 to 20 minutes.

7. Serve warm with tortilla chips or bread. Enjoy!

Turkish Red Lentil Soup

Total cooking & preparation time: 50 minutes

Servings: 4

Nutritional Value (Amount Per Serving)

188.2 Calories
10 Calories from Fat
1.2 g Total Fat
0.2 g Saturated Fat
0 mg Cholesterol
632.3 mg Sodium
33.6 g Total Carbohydrate
5.9 g Dietary Fiber
0.6 g Sugars
12.5 g Protein

Ingredients

- 4 cups stock, vegetable
- 1 cup red lentil, washed & cleaned
- 1/2 cup white potato, peeled & diced
- 1/4 cup onion, mild & finely chopped
- 1 tsp. paprika
- Salt & pepper, to taste

Cooking Directions

1. Use a colander to rinse the red lentils completely.

2. To remove the damaged beans or debris, sift through.

3. Put the lentils with the potatoes, stock, paprika and onions into a pot, preferably medium size. Let the mixture to boil and then decrease the heat settings.

4. Put a lid on the pot, loosely and to allow evaporation, leave the ajar slightly.

5. Cook until the lentils are tender, approximately half an hour.

6. Adjust pepper and salt to your taste.

7. Place approximately a cup of soup either into a food processor or blender & blend briefly.

8. Add the blended soup back to the pot with the reserved soup.

9. Heat through & serve warm.

Curried Lentils

Total cooking and preparation time: 35 minutes

Servings: 6

Nutritional Value (Amount Per Serving)

83.9 Calories
13 Calories from Fat
1.5 g Total Fat
0.2 g Saturated Fat
0 mg Cholesterol
552.5 mg Sodium
13.5 g Total Carbohydrate
5.3 g Dietary Fiber
2.8 g Sugars
6.4 g Protein

Ingredients

- 12 oz. fresh spinach leaves, washed & chopped
- 1 tbsp. ginger, fresh & grated
- 1 can plum tomatoes with liquid, chopped (14 oz.)
- 1 cup lentils, raw
- 3 tbsp. soy sauce
- 1 tbsp. curry powder
- 1/4 tsp. nutmeg
- 2 minced garlic cloves,
- 1 tsp. olive oil
- 1/4 tsp. cinnamon

Cooking Directions

1. Wash the lentils using cold water & sort. Cook approximately 5 to 10 minutes, until tender but firm.

2. Heat 4 cups of water approximately 10 minutes & 15 minutes on low or medium heat settings.

3. In a skillet, preferably large heat the olive oil.

4. Add the garlic, when the oil is hot and sauté approximately a minute, over moderately low heat settings and then add the spinach & cook until all the leaves are wilted, approximately two minutes or so.

5. Put the lentils with the leftover ingredients to the skillet.

6. Cover; simmer approximately 15 minutes, over very low heat.

7. You can try this with rice, couscous, or mashed potatoes.

Spinach-Garlic-Edamame Hummus

Total cooking and preparation time: 10 minutes

Servings: 4

Nutritional Value (Amount Per Serving)

641.2 Calories
389 Calories from Fat
43.3 g Total Fat
6 g Saturated Fat
0 mg Cholesterol
1968.5 mg Sodium
47.4 g Total Carbohydrate
13.1 g Dietary Fiber
0.5 g Sugars
23.5 g Protein

Ingredients

- 1 can garbanzo beans, drained (12 oz.)
- 1 small package spinach, frozen & chopped (approximately 1 cup)
- 1/2 cup tahini
- 6 garlic cloves (or as per your choice)
- 3/4 cup edamame, boiled & shells removed
- 1/4 to 1/2 cup olive oil
- 1 tbsp. red pepper flakes
- 2 tsp. sea salt

Cooking Directions

1. Combine everything together in a food processor.

2. To get the desired consistency, add olive oil (if you wish, you may even use "garbanzo beans juice", or water).

3. This is EVEN excellent with the leftover.

Thai Peanut

Total cooking and preparation: 25 minutes

Servings: 3

Nutritional Value (Amount Per Serving)

480.6 Calories
133 Calories from Fat
14.9 g Total Fat
2.8 g Saturated Fat
47.9 mg Cholesterol
1303.2 mg Sodium
70.1 g Total Carbohydrate
6.4 g Dietary Fiber
13.5 g Sugars
21.1 g Protein

Ingredients

- 1 1/2 cups broccoli, frozen or fresh, cut into pieces, preferably bite-sized
- 1/2 carrot, grated
- 2 tsp. garlic, minced
- 0.5 package fettuccine (approximately 8 oz.)
- 4 tbsp. soy sauce, low sodium
- 1/2 tsp. ginger, ground
- 1 tbsp. brown sugar
- 3 1/2 tbsp. rice wine vinegar
- 1/2 tsp. red pepper flakes
- 4 tbsp. peanut butter, reduced-fat

Cooking Directions

1. Prepare the fettuccini as mentioned on the package in a large pot. Add the broccoli into the pot towards the end of the pasta cooking and cook approximately 3 to 4 minutes.

2. Over medium high heat settings, heat the garlic in a greased saucepan, preferably large approximately 2 minutes.

3. Add brown sugar, ginger, & red pepper flakes into the saucepan and cook for two more minutes.

4. Add peanut butter, rice wine vinegar, & soy sauce to the saucepan. To make a sauce, mix in the peanut butter to the liquid and whisk using a spaghetti spoon.

5. Add the cooked broccoli / pasta to the saucepan as soon as the sauce starts to bubble. Add the carrot & mix well. To prevent any clumps, mix the mixture well.

6. Enjoy!

Mushrooms and Bell Peppers

Total cooking and preparation time: 20 minutes

Servings: 3 units

Nutritional Value (Amount Per Serving)

208 Calories
145 Calories from Fat
16.2 g Total Fat
2.3 g Saturated Fat
0 mg Cholesterol
1016.2 mg Sodium
11.6 g Total Carbohydrate
3.3 g Dietary Fiber
4.7 g Sugars
5.1 g Protein

Ingredients

- 1 cup mushrooms, champignon & sliced
- 3 garlic cloves, minced
- 2 bell peppers, deseeded & diced
- 1 tbsp. rice wine, Chinese
- 3 onions green & sliced
- 1 tsp. sesame oil
- 2 tbsp. olive oil
- 2 to 3 tbsp. soy sauce

Cooking Directions

1. Over medium high heat settings in a large skillet, heat the oil approximately 2 to 4 minutes.

2. Stir fry the onions approximately a minute and then add the garlic approximately half a minute.

3. Add mushrooms and peppers & stir-fry approximately 2 minutes, until a bit soft.

4. Add the soy sauce and wine & continue stirring approximately two minutes.

5. Remove from heat, when done and put the sesame sauce in the mixture. Mix well and serve warm.

Grilled Mushrooms

Total cooking and preparation time:25 minutes

Servings 4

Nutritional Value (Amount Per Serving)

64.6 Calories
52 Calories from Fat
5.9 g Total Fat
1.2 g Saturated Fat
0 mg Cholesterol
69.7 mg Sodium
2.2 g Total Carbohydrate
0.6 g Dietary Fiber
1.1 g Sugars
1.9 g Protein

Ingredients

- 1/2-pound medium size mushrooms, whole & fresh
- 1/2 tsp. dill weed
- 1/4 cup margarine, melted
- 1/2 tsp. garlic salt

Cooking Directions

1. Spread the mushrooms on a skewer.

2. Mix together the garlic salt, margarine, and dill and brush this over the mushrooms.

3. Over hot heat, grill approximately 10 to 15 minutes, basting & turning after every five minutes.

Lemon Herb Quinoa

Total cooking and preparation time: 30 minutes

Servings:6

Nutritional Value (Amount Per Serving)

137.1 Calories
46 Calories from Fat
5.2 g Total Fat
0.6 g Saturated Fat
0 mg Cholesterol
295.8 mg Sodium
18.9 g Total Carbohydrate
2.2 g Dietary Fiber
0.2 g Sugars
4.1 g Protein

Ingredients

- 3 tbsp. parsley, chopped
- 1 cup quinoa
- 3/4 tsp. oregano or 3/4 tsp. marjoram, dried
- 2 tbsp. lemon juice, fresh
- 1/2 tsp. lemon rind, fresh & grated
- 2 cups water
- 1/4 tsp. rosemary, dried & crumbled
- 1/2 tsp. thyme, dried
- 1 1/2 tbsp. vegetable oil
- 1/4 tsp. pepper
- 3/4 tsp. salt

Cooking Directions

1. In a bowl, preferably large, arrange the quinoa & use cold water to fill the bowl.

2. Use a strainer to drain & repeat the process approximately four more times.

3. In a saucepan, preferably 2-quart, heat the oil, over medium-high heat settings.

4. Add the rinsed quinoa & cook approximately 3 to 5 minutes, until the quinoa starts making a popping & cracking noise, stirring frequently.

5. Stir in the marjoram, water, rosemary, and thyme.

6. Let it boil and then decrease the heat settings. Simmer approximately 15 more minutes, covered.

7. Stir in the lemon juice, parsley, lemon rind, pepper and salt.

8. Simmer approximately five more minutes, covered.

9. Fluff using a fork.

Perfect Microwave Rice

Total cooking and preparation time: 27 mins

Servings: 6

Nutritional Value (Amount Per Serving)

233.5 Calories
12 Calories from Fat
1.4 g Total Fat
0.7 g Saturated Fat
2.5 mg Cholesterol
15.6 mg Sodium
49.3 g Total Carbohydrate
0.8 g Dietary Fiber
0.1 g Sugars
4.4 g Protein

Ingredients

- 3 1/2 cups homemade stock or 3 1/2 cups canned broth or 3 1/2 cups water
- 2 cups rice, preferably long grain
- 1 1/2 tsp. olive oil or 1 1/2 tsp. butter
- salt

Cooking Directions

1. In a microwave safe bowl, preferably large, put everything together except the salt.

2. During cooking, rice normally gets double in size so go for a large container to accommodate the final product.

3. Microwave on high settings, approximately 10 minutes, uncovered.

4. Then on medium-low settings approximately 15 minutes, uncovered.

5. During the cooking process, don't stir the rice at anytime.

6. Season with salt & just before serving, fluff using a fork.

Creamy Chickpea Curry

Total cooking and preparation time: 25 mins

Servings: 4

Nutritional Value (Amount Per Serving)

752.6 Calories
222 Calories from Fat
24.8 g Total Fat
16.6 g Saturated Fat
0 mg Cholesterol
869.5 mg Sodium
122.8 g Total Carbohydrate
7.6 g Dietary Fiber
57.1 g Sugars
11.7 g Protein

Ingredients

- 1 can chickpeas, drained (approximately 15 oz.)
- 1 onion, medium & chopped
- 4 cups jasmine rice, cooked
- 1 tbsp. red curry paste
- 2 tbsp. soy sauce
- 1 tomatoes, medium & chopped
- 3 garlic cloves, large & minced
- 1 tbsp. brown sugar
- 1 tbsp. lime juice, fresh
- 1/4 cup basil, fresh & chopped or 2 tbsp. cilantro, chopped
- 1 can coconut milk (approximately 13 1/2 oz.)
- 2 tbsp. oil

Cooking Directions

1. Over a medium high heat setting in a large skillet, heat the oil.

2. Add onions & cook until brown, approximately one to two minutes.

3. Add curry and garlic.

4. Stir-fry until curry is completely dissolved and garlic becomes soft.

5. Add Coconut Milk, soy sauce & chickpeas.

6. Bring the mixture to a boil & simmer approximately 10 minutes.

7. Add lime juice, sugar, and tomatoes and simmer for five more minutes.

8. Stir in cilantro or basil until combined & serve over the rice.

Fluffy Vegan Pancakes

Total cooking and preparation time: 20 mins

Servings: 4

Nutritional Value (Amount Per Serving)

353.8 Calories
85 Calories from Fat
9.5 g Total Fat
1.2 g Saturated Fat
0 mg Cholesterol
468.6 mg Sodium
55.6 g Total Carbohydrate
2.4 g Dietary Fiber
5 g Sugars
10.4 g Protein

Ingredients

- 1 tsp. baking powder
- 2 cups flour
- 2 cups soymilk
- 1 tsp. baking soda
- 2 tbsp. oil

Cooking Directions

1. In a large bowl, sift together the flour, baking powder & baking soda.

2. Add oil and soymilk; mix until "mixed well".

3. Toss in any extras chocolate chips, blueberries and so on that you might want.

4. Over medium heat, heat a skillet, lightly oiled.

5. Drop batter (2 to 3 tbsp.) into the skillet & cover.

6. When the middle starts bubbling, flip & cover it again.

7. While you are about to finish the others, put the made pancakes in oven at 100 C/200 F.

Sautéed Green Beans & Red Onion

Total cooking and preparation time:30min

Servings: 4

Nutritional Value (Amount Per Serving)

108.5 Calories
63 Calories from Fat
7 g Total Fat
1 g Saturated Fat
0 mg Cholesterol
591.8 mg Sodium
11 g Total Carbohydrate
3.6 g Dietary Fiber
5.3 g Sugars
2.4 g Protein

Ingredients

- 1 red onion, medium & cut into wedges, preferably ½"
- 1 pound green beans, trimmed & halved
- 2 tsp. balsamic vinegar
- 1/4 tsp. pepper, ground
- 2 tbsp. olive oil
- 1 cup water
- 1 tsp. coarse salt

Cooking Directions

1. Over medium heat in a large skillet, bring oil, 1 cup water, pepper, and salt to a simmer.

2. Add the onion & green beans. Cover; cook approximately 8 to 10 minutes, until the beans are tender, but still crisp.

3. Uncover, continue cooking approximately 5 to 8 more minutes, until beans are tender, water has evaporated & onions become brown, stirring frequently.

4. Stir in vinegar & serve.

Thai Style Butternut Squash Soup

Total cooking and preparation time: 30min

Servings: 2

Nutritional Value (Amount Per Serving)

717.3 Calories
434 Calories from Fat
48.3 g Total Fat
37.3 g Saturated Fat
0 mg Cholesterol
50.4 mg Sodium
77.4 g Total Carbohydrate
12.6 g Dietary Fiber
14.8 g Sugars
10.3 g Protein

Ingredients

- 1 can of coconut milk, (approximately 13 1/2 oz.)
- 1 butternut squash, cut into chunks (peeled & deseeded)
- 1-pint stock, vegetable
- 1 tsp. curry powder
- 1 red onion, chopped
- 1 tbsp. olive oil
- Pepper & salt

Cooking Directions

1. In a pan, heavy based heat the olive oil & cook the onion approximately two to three minutes, until soft.

2. Add the curry powder, butternut squash & stock to taste.

3. Bring the mixture to a boil & then cover; simmer for few minutes, until the squash becomes tender.

4. Stir the coconut milk in, once the squash is cooked.

5. Pour into a liquidizer/food processer & blend until smooth, for few minutes.

6. Return to the pan & warm through.

7. Just before serving, season pepper & salt to taste.

Mint Limeade

Total cooking and preparation time: 20 mins

Servings: 8

Nutritional Value (Amount Per Serving)

178.6 Calories
0 Calories from Fat
0 g Total Fat
0 g Saturated Fat
0 mg Cholesterol
7.5 mg Sodium
46.6 g Total Carbohydrate
0.4 g Dietary Fiber
44.2 g Sugars
0.2 g Protein

Ingredients

- 1 cup lime juice, fresh (approximately 12 limes)
- 1/3 cup mint, fresh & coarsely chopped
- 13/4 cups Splenda sugar substitute, or 1 3/4 cups sugar or less to taste
- 10 mint sprigs & 10 lime slices, to garnish
- 6 cups water, divided

Cooking Directions

1. In a small saucepan, mix together chopped mint, 2 cups water & sugar; let it starts boiling.

2. Cook for few minutes, until sugar dissolves, stirring frequently. Take the saucepan away from the heat & let stand approximately 10 minutes.

3. Strain through a strainer into a bowl, discarding the solids.

4. In a large pitcher, mix together the leftover lime juice, 4 cups water, and sugar syrup, stirring well.

5. Serve over ice and if desired, garnish with lime slices and mint sprigs.

Chickpea Cutlets

Total cooking and preparation time: 27 mins

Servings: 4

Nutritional Value (Amount Per Serving)

193.6 Calories
73 Calories from Fat
8.2 g Total Fat
1.2 g Saturated Fat
0 mg Cholesterol
781.7 mg Sodium
24.6 g Total Carbohydrate
3.6 g Dietary Fiber
1 g Sugars
5.9 g Protein

Ingredients

- 1/2 tsp. Hungarian paprika
- 2 tbsp. soy sauce
- 1/2 tsp. lemon zest
- 1 cup chickpeas, cooked
- 1/2 cup breadcrumbs, plain
- 2 garlic cloves, grated or pressed
- 1/4 cup water or 1/4 cup vegetable broth
- 1/2 tsp. dried thyme
- 1/4 tsp. rubbed sage, dried
- 2 tbsp. olive oil & more for pan frying
- 1/2 cup vital wheat gluten

Cooking Directions

1. Mash the chickpeas with oil together until no complete chickpeas stay behind.

2. Add the leftover ingredients & knead approximately three to five minutes, until the strings of gluten have formed.

3. Over medium heat settings, preheat a large skillet, preferably nonstick.

4. Divide the dough into equal pieces, preferably 4. Flatten each piece & stretch to 4x6", roughly.

5. Put a small quantity of olive oil to the pan and place the cutlets. Cook approximately 6 to 7 mins on each side until they are firm to the touch and lightly brown.

Vegan Bacon

Total cooking and preparation time: 25 min

Servings: 4

Nutritional Value (Amount Per Serving)

179.2 Calories
103 Calories from Fat
11.5 g Total Fat
2 g Saturated Fat
0 mg Cholesterol
692.6 mg Sodium
6.5 g Total Carbohydrate
3.6 g Dietary Fiber
1.1 g Sugars
16.9 g Protein

Ingredients

- 1 tsp. liquid smoke
- 1-pound firm tofu, cut into strips
- 2 tbsp. soya sauce
- 1 tbsp. oil, not olive oil
- 2 tbsp. nutritional yeast

Cooking Directions

1. Over low heat settings, fry the tofu strips approximately 10 minutes, until crispy on the outside.

2. Turn the strips & fry on the other side as well, approximately 10 more minutes.

3. Mix the liquid smoke with the soya sauce first, then remove the pan from the heat.

4. Put the soya sauce/liquid smoke into the pan & stir the tofu. Make sure that all sides of the tofu are evenly coated with the mixture.

5. Sprinkle the yeast all over, over the heat, stir some more, until the tofu is covered with sticky yeast & the liquid is absorbed.

Crispy Baked Radish Chips

Total cooking and preparation time: 20 mins

Servings: 4

Nutritional Value (Amount Per Serving)

3.6 Calories
0 Calories from Fat
0 g Total Fat
0 g Saturated Fat
0 mg Cholesterol
8.8 mg Sodium
0.8 g Total Carbohydrate
0.4 g Dietary Fiber
0.4 g Sugars
0.2 g Protein

Ingredients

- 10 to 15 radishes, large
- Pepper & salt, to taste
- Cooking spray, nonstick

Cooking Directions

1. Preheat your oven to 375 F/190 C.

2. Slice the radishes into chips, preferably very thin & spread them on a cookie sheet (sprayed with the cooking spray).

3. Using cooking spray, lightly mist the radish slices and then sprinkle with pepper and salt.

4. Bake approximately 10 minutes. Flip & bake until crispy, approximately 5 to 10 minutes more.

Garlic Quinoa

Total cooking and preparation time: 25minutes

Servings: 4

Nutritional Value (Amount Per Serving)

196.3 Calories
53 Calories from Fat
6 g Total Fat
0.8 g Saturated Fat
0 mg Cholesterol
152.1 mg Sodium
29.6 g Total Carbohydrate
3.3 g Dietary Fiber
0.9 g Sugars
6.3 g Protein

Ingredients

- 2 cups broth or 2 cups water
- 1 cup quinoa, rinsed & drained well
- 2 tsp. garlic, minced
- 1⁄2 cup onion, chopped
- 1 tbsp. olive oil
- 1⁄4 tsp. salt, or to taste

Cooking Directions

1. In a large pan, heat the olive oil & sauté the onion approximately 3 to 4 minutes. Add the garlic & continue sautéing for half a minute more.

2. Add quinoa, salt and water to the pan and bring the mixture to a boil then decrease the heat settings.

3. Cover; simmer until liquid is absorbed, approximately 15 minutes.

Raw Apple Crumble

Total cooking and preparation time: 20min

Servings: 10

Nutritional Value (Amount Per Serving)

306.2 Calories
140 Calories from Fat
15.6 g Total Fat
1.5 g Saturated Fat
0 mg Cholesterol
32.8 mg Sodium
44 g Total Carbohydrate
6.4 g Dietary Fiber
32 g Sugars
4.8 g Protein

Ingredients

- 1 cup raisins, soaked & drained
- 8 apples, peeled & chopped
- 1 cup dates, pitted
- 1/4 tsp. nutmeg
- 1 tsp. cinnamon
- 2 tbsp. lemon juice
- 1 tsp. cinnamon
- 2 cups walnuts
- 1/8 tsp. salt

Cooking Directions

1. Place nutmeg, raisins, cinnamon & 2 apples in a food processor and process until smooth, to make the filling.

2. Place the leftover chopped apples & the lemon juice in a bowl, toss well.

3. Put the pureed filling mixture over the top, mixing well.

4. In a lasagna pan, preferably medium sized, spoon the apple mixture and keep it aside.

5. Pulse dates, walnuts, salt and cinnamon in a food processor until coarsely ground, for crumble.

6. Don't over mix.

7. Using your hands, crumble the mixture over the apples & press lightly.

8. For additional flavors, let it marinate approximately two to three hours or serve immediately.

Fiesta Cucumber & Corn Salad

Total cooking and preparation time: 25 min

Servings: 4

Nutritional Value (Amount Per Serving)

107.9 Calories
10 Calories from Fat
1.1 g Total Fat
0.2 g Saturated Fat
0 mg Cholesterol
483.1 mg Sodium
24.8 g Total Carbohydrate
3.7 g Dietary Fiber
8.4 g Sugars
3.8 g Protein

Ingredients

- 1 can whole kernel corn, drained (8 3/4 oz.)
- 1/4 to 1/2 cup cilantro, fresh & chopped
- 1 cucumber, seeded & chopped
- 1/2 cup each green & red bell pepper, chopped
- 1 can stewed tomatoes, drained & chopped (16 oz.)
- 1/2 tsp. cumin
- 1 tsp. red pepper flakes, crushed
- 4 tsp. white wine vinegar
- 1 clove garlic, minced
- Pepper and salt, to taste

Cooking Directions

1. In a glass bowl, toss everything together.

2. Before serving, cover & let it chill for a minimum period of half an hour or refrigerator for overnight, stirring occasionally.

Carrot Rice with Peanuts

Total cooking and preparation time: 30min

Servings: 6

Nutritional Value (Amount Per Serving)

199 Calories
61 Calories from Fat
6.9 g Total Fat
1.9 g Saturated Fat
5.1 mg Cholesterol
109.6 mg Sodium
30 g Total Carbohydrate
1.9 g Dietary Fiber
2 g Sugars
4.8 g Protein

Ingredients

- 1 tsp. minced gingerroot
- 1/4 cup roasted peanuts
- 1 onion, thinly sliced
- 3/4 cup grated carrot
- 1 cup rice, long-grain or basmati
- Cilantro, fresh & chopped to garnish
- Pepper & salt, to taste
- 2 cups water
- 1 tbsp. butter

Cooking Directions

1. In a saucepan, preferably medium sized, mix water and rice together. Over high heat settings, let the mixture to boil.

2. Decrease the heat settings to low, cover with lid & let it steam approximately 20 minutes, until cooked/tender.

3. Pulverize the peanuts in a blender & keep it aside, while the rice is still cooking.

4. Over medium-high heat in a large skillet, melt the butter & sauté onions for few minutes, until golden brown.

5. Stir in carrots, ginger, & salt to taste.

6. Decrease the heat settings to low. Cover; steam approximately 5 minutes.

7. Stir in the peanuts & pepper.

8. Add rice to the skillet, when done & gently stir to combine with remaining ingredients.

9. Garnish with cilantro (fresh & chopped) and serve hot.

Vegan Banana Muffins

Total cooking and preparation time: 30 min

Servings: 12

Nutritional Value (Amount Per Serving)

242.3 Calories
86 Calories from Fat
9.6 g Total Fat
1.3 g Saturated Fat
0 mg Cholesterol
284 mg Sodium
37.5 g Total Carbohydrate
2.7 g Dietary Fiber
13.8 g Sugars
3.4 g Protein

Ingredients

- 1/2 cup pure maple syrup or brown sugar
- 1 tsp. baking powder
- 4 bananas, ripe
- 1 tsp. cinnamon
- 3/4 tsp. salt
- 1 tsp. cardamom powder
- 1/2 cup vegetable oil
- 1 cup flour, whole wheat
- 1 1/2 cups white flour
- 1 tsp. baking soda

Cooking Directions

1. Preheat your oven to 350 F/ 175 C.

2. Arrange the cups in tin approximately 12 muffins.

3. In a bowl, mash the bananas.

4. Add oil, maple syrup or sugar, salt, cardamom & cinnamon; mix well.

5. Add flours, baking soda & baking powder and mix.

6. Spoon into muffin tins & bake until muffins slightly browned on top and are done, approximately half an hour.

Seasoned Potatoes

Total cooking and preparation time: 30min

Servings: 4

Nutritional Value (Amount Per Serving)

179.1 Calories
18 Calories from Fat
2.1 g Total Fat
0.3 g Saturated Fat
0 mg Cholesterol
516.1 mg Sodium
36.3 g Total Carbohydrate
4.6 g Dietary Fiber
4 g Sugars
5.2 g Protein

Ingredients

- 2 scallions, large & finely chopped
- 1 tsp. garlic, finely chopped
- 2 potatoes, large & French fry cut
- 2 tsp. sesame seeds
- 2 tbsp. soy sauce
- 1 tsp. sesame oil
- 2 tsp. sugar

Cooking Directions

1. Arrange the cut potatoes in a large pot. Cover with enough water, put lid on pot & let it boil. Simmer until fork tender, approximately 10 minutes.

2. Add the leftover ingredients, in a mixing bowl, medium size.

3. Drain the liquid from the potatoes, when done & add potatoes to the seasoning. Mix well to evenly coat & serve immediately.

Lemon Asparagus

Total cooking and preparation time: 17 min

Servings: 2

Nutritional Value (Amount Per Serving)

100.2 Calories
46 Calories from Fat
5.1 g Total Fat
0.8 g Saturated Fat
0 mg Cholesterol
323.3 mg Sodium
12.6 g Total Carbohydrate
5.6 g Dietary Fiber
3.7 g Sugars
5.8 g Protein

Ingredients

- 1 tbsp. oregano, fresh & chopped or 1 tsp. oregano, dried
- 1-pound asparagus, tough ends trimmed
- 1 lemon, sliced thinly
- 1⁄4 tsp. pepper, fresh & ground
- 2 tsp. olive oil, extra virgin
- 1⁄4 tsp. salt

Cooking Directions

1. Preheat your oven to 450 F/225 C.

2. In a rimmed baking sheet, preferably large, mix together the lemon slices, asparagus, oil, oregano, pepper and salt, toss well. Roast approximately 13 to 15 minutes, until the asparagus is crisp - tender, shake occasionally to toss.

3. Let it cool at room temperature and then serve or hot.

Barking Cauliflower

Total cooking and preparation time: 22 min

Servings 5

Nutritional Value (Amount Per Serving)

87.6 Calories
39 Calories from Fat
4.4 g Total Fat
0.6 g Saturated Fat
0 mg Cholesterol
308.1 mg Sodium
10.8 g Total Carbohydrate
3.7 g Dietary Fiber
3.5 g Sugars
3.3 g Protein

Ingredients

- 1 tsp. basil, dried
- 1 slice whole wheat bread or white bread, processed into fresh crumbs
- 1⁄2 tsp. thyme, dried
- 1 1⁄2 pounds' cauliflower, cut into florets
- 4 cloves garlic, minced
- 1⁄2 tsp. marjoram, dried
- 1 1⁄2 tbsp. olive oil, divided
- Pepper
- 1⁄2 tsp. salt

Cooking Directions

1. Steam the cauliflower approximately 5 minutes, until just tender (leaving few crunches in it), remove & keep it warm.

2. In the meantime, mix together the crumbs with herbs, pepper & salt.

3. Over medium high heat settings in a skillet, heat a tbsp of oil & add the garlic, sauté for few minutes, until the garlic is golden.

4. Now, stir the crumbs in.

5. Toss the crumb mixture with the leftover oil & the cauliflower.

6. Serve.

Soba Noodles

Total cooking and preparation time: 25min

Servings 8

Nutritional Value (Amount Per Serving)

328.4 Calories
105 Calories from Fat
11.7 g Total Fat
1.7 g Saturated Fat
0 mg Cholesterol
958.1 mg Sodium
49.9 g Total Carbohydrate
1.5 g Dietary Fiber
4.2 g Sugars
11 g Protein

Ingredients

- 1-pound vermicelli or 1 pound soba noodles
- 1 cup onion, green & sliced
- 1/4 cup soy sauce
- 2 tbsp. balsamic vinegar
- 1/4 cup sesame oil
- 2 tbsp. chili oil
- 1/2 cup sesame seeds, toasted
- 2 tbsp. sugar

Cooking Directions

1. Cook the noodles as per the directions, drain & rinse.

2. Add sauce, stir well & let the noodles soak in.

3. Sprinkle with green onions & sesame seeds.

Za'atar Tomatoes

Total cooking and preparation time: 20 min

Servings: 4

Nutritional Value (Amount Per Serving)

92.4 Calories
63 Calories from Fat
7.1 g Total Fat
1 g Saturated Fat
0 mg Cholesterol
9.2 mg Sodium
7.1 g Total Carbohydrate
2.2 g Dietary Fiber
4.8 g Sugars
1.6 g Protein

Ingredients

* 4 beefsteak tomatoes, large & ripe
* 2 tbsp. spice mix, za'atar
* 2 tbsp. olive oil, extra virgin

Cooking Directions

1. Preheat your oven to 400 F/200 C.

2. Core the tomatoes & slice them into thick rounds.

3. Arrange the tomatoes in a single layer on a baking sheet, preferably large sided. Drizzle a small quantity of olive oil on each tomato & sprinkle za'atar over the top.

4. Bake until hot but not mushy or approximately 10 minutes.

Chapter Seven: Dinner

Spinach with Pine Nuts

Total cooking and preparation time: 12 min

Servings: 2

Nutritional Value (Amount Per Serving)

180.1 Calories
137 Calories from Fat
15.3 g Total Fat
1.9 g Saturated Fat
0 mg Cholesterol
717.4 mg Sodium
8.9 g Total Carbohydrate
4.4 g Dietary Fiber
1.1 g Sugars
6.1 g Protein

Ingredients

1. 1 bag spinach, (12 oz.)
2. 1 tsp. red pepper flakes
3. 2 to 3 minced garlic cloves
4. 1 1/2 tbsp. pine nuts
5. 2 tsp. water
6. 1/2 tsp. black pepper, fresh & ground
7. 1 1 /2 tbsp. olive oil
8. 1/2 tsp. salt

Cooking Directions

1. On medium high heat settings in a skillet, heat the olive oil and add garlic & water.

2. Add spinach to the skillet, once hot. Sprinkle with black pepper & salt. Stir & cook for few minutes, until spinach is wilted.

3. Adjust the heat settings to low or let it simmer for some time and then put the pine nuts. Cook approximately a minute, covered. If desired, add the red pepper flakes. Cook for an additional minute.

4. Enjoy!

Tomato Basil Soup

Total cooking and preparation time: 12 mins

Servings: 3

Nutritional Value (Amount Per Serving)

83.9 Calories
43 Calories from Fat
4.9 g Total Fat
0.7 g Saturated Fat
0 mg Cholesterol
9.1 m Sodium
9.6 Total Carbohydrate
2.4 g Dietary Fiber
5.2 g Sugars
2 g Protein

Ingredients

- 5 cups vegetable stock
- 1 can tomatoes, peeled & ground (14 1/2 oz.)
- 2 crushed cloves garlic
- 1/2 cup thinly sliced basil, fresh & loosely packed
- 1 sweet onion, medium & chopped
- Black pepper, freshly ground & salt
- 1 tbsp. olive oil

Cooking Directions

1. Over medium high heat settings in a large soup pot, heat the olive oil.

2. Add the garlic and onion & cook, approximately 10 minutes, until softened, don't burn the garlic, stirring frequently.

3. Add the stock & tomatoes.

4. Bring to a boil & then decrease the heat settings and let it simmer.

5. Cook approximately 20 minutes, until soup is thickened slightly.

6. Season with pepper & salt and then stir in the basil.

7. Place the soup pot directly in a sink & blend until smooth using a stick blender.

8. Serve immediately.

Chickpea Curry

Total cooking and preparation time: 15 minutes

Servings: 2

Nutritional Value (Amount Per Serving)

437.6 Calories
148 Calories from Fat
16.4 g Total Fat
2.2 g Saturated Fat
0 mg Cholesterol
1267 mg Sodium
62 g Total Carbohydrate
12.2 g Dietary Fiber
4.1 g Sugars
13 g Protein

Ingredients

- 1 can chickpeas, drained & rinsed (16 ounce)
- 5 minced garlic cloves
- 1 tsp. ginger, fresh & minced
- 1 to 4 tsp. curry powder
- 1 onion, diced
- water
- 1 tomatoes, medium & diced
- 2 to 3 tbsp. olive oil
- 1/2 tsp. salt

Cooking Directions

1. Over medium high heat settings in a large skillet, heat the oil and sauté the onions approximately three minutes.

2. Add curry powder, garlic & ginger, stir & cook for an additional minute.

3. Add chickpeas, a tbsp. of water & salt.

4. Cook & stir approximately a minute.

5. Add the tomatoes & cook approximately five minutes, stirring gently.

6. If it's sticking or burning or if it seems dry, add an additional spoonful of water.

7. Serve with rice and flatbread.

Roasted Baby Red Potatoes

Total cooking and preparation time: 50 minutes

Servings 4

Nutritional Value (Amount Per Serving)

117.2 Calories
31 Calories from Fat
3.5 g Total Fat
0.5 g Saturated Fat
0 mg Cholesterol
7.7 mg Sodium
19.8 g Total Carbohydrate
2.6 g Dietary Fiber
1.9 g Sugars
2.6 g Protein

Ingredients

- 1/2 tsp. basil, dried
- 3/4 pound baby red potato, washed, quartered
- 10 garlic cloves, medium & peeled
- 1/2 red onion, large & cut in chunks, preferably ½"
- Pepper and salt
- 1/2 bell pepper, medium & cut in chunks, preferably ½"
- 1 tbsp. olive oil

Cooking Directions

1. Preheat your oven to 225 C /450 F.

2. Using non-stick cooking spray, spray an oven-proof dish and add the vegetables, drizzle olive oil and toss well to evenly coat.

3. Sprinkle with salt and pepper to taste.

4. Place the dish in an oven & bake approximately 15 minutes, stir & return to the oven until potatoes are just tender, approximately 15 more minutes.

5. Sprinkle with basil, dried and if required, adjust pepper and salt to your taste, before serving, cover & allow standing, approximately 5 to 10 minutes.

Sesame Bok Choy

Total cooking and preparation time: 13 min

Servings 4

Nutritional Value (Amount Per Serving)

75.6 Calories
24 Calories from Fat
2.7 g Total Fat
0.3 g Saturated Fat
0 mg Cholesterol
516.2 mg Sodium
9.8 g Total Carbohydrate
2.7 g Dietary Fiber
6.2 g Sugars
4.4 g Protein

Ingredients

- 1 head bok choy
- 1 tbsp. rice wine
- 1 1/2 tbsp. regular or light soy sauce
- 1 tbsp. brown sugar
- 1/3 cup onion, green & chopped
- 1 tsp. canola oil
- 1/2 tsp. ginger, ground
- 1 tbsp. sesame seeds

Cooking Directions

1. Wash the bok choy using cold water. Cut the stems & tops into pieces, preferably 1".

2. Mix together the remaining ingredients in a bowl, preferably large & mix well.

3. Add the bok choy to the dressing & toss to evenly coat.

4. Place in a large pan or hot wok & stir-fry until desired tenderness is reached, approximately 8 to 10 minutes, over med-high heat.

Easy Vegan Pancakes

Total cooking and preparation time: 20 min

Servings 4

Nutritional Value (Amount Per Serving)

424.3 Calories
61 Calories from Fat
6.8 g Total Fat
0.9 g Saturated Fat
0 mg Cholesterol
1205.1 mg Sodium
77.1 g Total Carbohydrate
3 g Dietary Fiber
12.6 g Sugars
13 g Protein

Ingredients

- 2 and ½ cups flour, all-purpose
- 2 and ½ cups water or soymilk
- 2 tbsp. baking powder
- 2 tbsp. sugar
- 1 dash cinnamon
- 1 tbsp. vegetable oil
- 1 tsp. salt

Cooking Directions

1. Lightly mix all of the ingredients in a large bowl, until just combined, don't over mix.

2. Leave the mixture to rest on the counter approximately 5 minutes. To ensure that the batter is reasonably well incorporated, fold it onto itself 2 or 3 times, lightly.

3. Over medium high heat settings on a griddle or greased skillet, cook until golden.

4. While the pancakes are cooking, carefully break the large lumps apart, if any using the spatula.

5. Serve immediately.

Indian Spiced Rice

Total cooking and preparation time: 50 min

Servings 8

Nutritional Value (Amount Per Serving)

122.6 Calories
10 Calories from Fat
1.2 g Total Fat
0.7 g Saturated Fat
2.5 mg Cholesterol
158.2 mg Sodium
25 g Total Carbohydrate
0.5 g Dietary Fiber
0.1 g Sugars
2.3 g Protein

Ingredients

2 tsp. margarine or butter
1/4 cup onion, green & sliced
1/2 tsp. garam masala
1 1/3 cups rice, long grain
1 garlic clove, minced
1/8 tsp. red pepper, ground
2 2/3 cups water
1/2 tsp. salt

Cooking Directions

1. Over medium high heat settings in a saucepan, melt the butter and cook the green onion until golden & tender, don't burn them.

2. Stir in garam masala, rice, salt, garlic and red pepper. Cook and stir approximately a minute, over medium heat settings.

3. Add water to the saucepan and let it boil. Decrease the heat settings & simmer approximately 15 minutes; covered.

4. Remove the saucepan from the heat & let stand for 10 minutes, covered.

5. Place the prepared rice in a freezer bag, pushing out as much air as you possibly can. Seal, label & freeze.

6. Defrost in a fridge. Place in baking dish & add one tbsp. of water for each cup of rice. Stir & reheat at 150C/300 F approximately half an hour.

Hummus

Total cooking and preparation time: 5 min

Servings: 16

Nutritional Value (Amount Per Serving)

73.1 Calories
32 Calories from Fat
3.6 g Total Fat
0.5 g Saturated Fat
0 mg Cholesterol
238.9 mg Sodium
8.5 g Total Carbohydrate
1.8 g Dietary Fiber
0.1 g Sugars
2.4 g Protein

Ingredients

- 1 tsp. parsley, fresh & minced
- 2 cups garbanzo beans, canned, rinsed & drained
- 1 tbsp. olive oil, and more if needed
- 1/4 cup lemon juice
- 1 pinch paprika
- 2 garlic cloves, minced
- 1/3 cup tahini
- 1 tsp. salt

Cooking Directions

1. Place the lemon juice, tahini, garbanzo beans, garlic & salt in a food processor or blender. Blend until smooth, for few minutes.

2. To make a smooth mixture, put the olive oil into a feed tube at the garbanzo bean mixture.

3. Transfer this mixture to a large serving bowl.

4. If required, add more quantity of oil.

5. Sprinkle with parsley and paprika.

Creamy Chickpea and Tahini Casserole

Total cooking and preparation time: 55 min

Servings 6

Nutritional Value (Amount Per Serving)

354.5 Calories
6.3 g Total Fat
0.9 g Saturated Fat
0 mg Cholesterol
438.8 mg Sodium
64.4 g Total Carbohydrate
10.8 g Dietary Fiber
4.3 g Sugars
12.1 g Protein

Ingredients

- 1 white onion, medium & chopped
- 3 to 4 cups cooked brown rice
- 1 can tomatoes, diced & un-drained (28 oz.)
- 2 cans chickpeas, drained & rinsed (15 to 22 1/2 oz.)
- 1 tsp. oregano, dried
- 3 tbsp. water
- 1 to 2 tsp. parsley, dried
- 3 tbsp. tahini
- 1 tsp. garlic powder (or equiv. fresh garlic)
- 1 tbsp. sesame seeds, toasted
- 1 tsp. basil, dried

Cooking Directions

1. Preheat your oven to 375 F/185 C.

2. Mix water & tahini until well mixed & fluffy. Keep it aside.

3. Spray a pan, preferably 9x13 with olive oil.

4. Dump all of the ingredients into the pan.

5. Add pepper and salt to taste, mixing well.

6. Add the tahini mixture, stirring well until combined.

7. Bake at 185 C/375 F until top begins to brown, approximately half an hour.

8. Sprinkle sesame seeds & bake approximately five more minutes.

9. Serve hot!

Creamy Fruit Salad

Total cooking and preparation time: 35 minutes

Servings 10

Nutritional Value (Amount Per Serving)

118.8 Calories
20 Calories from Fat
2.3 g Total Fat
0.2 g Saturated Fat
0 mg Cholesterol
2.5 mg Sodium
26.4 g Total Carbohydrate
3.6 g Dietary Fiber
18.6 g Sugars
1.4 g Protein

Ingredients

- 1 box instant vanilla pudding mix, sugar-free (1 and ½ oz.)
- 2 apples, medium & diced
- 1 can pineapple tidbits, drained & juice reserved (20 oz.)
- 2 bananas, medium & diced
- 1/4 cup chopped pecans
- 2 cups strawberries, sliced
- Juice of 1 lemon
- 2 cups grapes
- vanilla pudding mix
- 1/2 cup water

Cooking Directions

1. In a large mixing bowl, mix together the bananas, lemon juice & apples. Toss until coated evenly.

2. Add strawberries, pineapple, pecans & grapes.

3. Combine pineapple juice, pudding mix & water in a small mixing bowl, whisk with a wire for few minutes, until smooth.

4. Add the pudding mixture to the fruit.

5. Gently mix both the mixtures until thoroughly coated.

6. Store at a low temperature until ready to serve.

Cheese Pasta

Total cooking and preparation time: 15 min

Servings 3

Nutritional Value (Amount Per Serving)

99.7 Calories
8 Calories from Fat
0.9 g Total Fat
0.1 g Saturated Fat
0 mg Cholesterol
388.8 mg Sodium
17.6 g Total Carbohydrate
3.7 g Dietary Fiber
0 g Sugars
7.9 g Protein

Ingredients

- macaroni noodles or tortilla chips
- 1/4 cup nutritional yeast flakes
- 1 can tomatoes, diced with green chilies
- 1/4 cup flour
- 1 -2 tbsp. mayonnaise, vegan
- 1/4-1/2 tsp. pepper
- paprika
- 1 cup of water
- cayenne pepper

Cooking Directions

1. Sift the dry ingredients together in a medium saucepan.

2. Over medium heat, whisk the ingredients in water until bubbly.

3. Stir in tomatoes and margarine.

4. Continue cooking until well heated.

5. You may serve this over noodles for Mac & cheese, or over chips for nachos.

Spicy Hash Browns

Total cooking and preparation time: 45 min

Servings 5

Nutritional Value (Amount Per Serving)

226.8 Calories
51 Calories from Fat
5.7 g Total Fat
0.8 g Saturated Fat
0 mg Cholesterol
247.7 mg Sodium
41.3 g Total Carbohydrate
4 g Dietary Fiber
1.8 g Sugars
3.9 g Protein

Ingredients

- 6 and a 1/2 cups baking potatoes, diced (approximately 2 and a 1/2 pounds)
- 1/8 tsp. black pepper
- 1 tsp. paprika
- 1/4 tsp. red pepper, ground
- cooking spray
- 3/4 tsp. chili powder
- 2 tbsp. olive oil
- 1/2 tsp. salt

Cooking Directions

1. Preheat your oven to 400 F/ 200 C.

2. In a large bowl, mix together the olive oil, chili powder, paprika, red peppers, salt & black pepper; stirring well.

3. Add the potatoes & stir well to evenly coat.

4. Arrange the potatoes on a cookie sheet coated with cooking spray, in a single layer.

5. Bake at 400 F /200 C until browned, approximately half an hour.

Garden vegetable soup

Total cooking and preparation time: 35 min

Servings: 4

Nutritional Value (Amount Per Serving)

42.2 Calories
4 Calories from Fat
0.4 g Total Fat
0.2 g Saturated Fat
0.3 mg Cholesterol
658.2 mg Sodium
8.8 g Total Carbohydrate
2.3 g Dietary Fiber
4.5 g Sugars
1.9 g Protein

Ingredients

- 3 cups vegetable broth, fat free
- 2/3 cup sliced carrot
- 1 tbsp. tomato paste
- 1/2 cup onion, diced
- 1/2 cup beans, green
- 1 1/2 cups cabbage, green & diced
- 1/2 tsp. basil, dried
- 1/4 tsp. oregano, dried
- 2 cloves garlic, minced
- 1/2 cup zucchini, dried
- 1/4 tsp. salt

Cooking Directions

1. Using non-stick cooking spray, spray a saucepan, preferably large.

2. Over low heat settings, sauté the carrot, garlic & onion approximately 5 minutes, until softened.

3. Add tomato paste, broth, green beans, and cabbage. Let it simmer until beans are tender, approximately 15 minutes, covered.

4. Stir in the zucchini & heat approximately five minutes.

5. Serve hot.

Fat Free Asian Salad Dressing

Total Cooking and Preparation Time: 5 min

Servings: 4

Nutritional Value (Amount Per Serving)

72.9 Calories
25 Calories from Fat
2.8 g Total Fat
0.4 g Saturated Fat
0 mg Cholesterol
1197.2 mg Sodium
5.1 g Total Carbohydrate
0.2 g Dietary Fiber
3.5 g Sugars
2.4 g Protein

Ingredients

- 3 drops sesame oil
- 1-piece ginger, fresh
- 2 garlic cloves
- 1 and a 1/2 oz. red wine vinegar
- 3 oz. soy sauce
- 1 tbsp. sugar
- 1/2 oz. water

Cooking Directions

1. Mince the ginger and garlic finely & whip together the remaining ingredients with a wire whisk.

2. Serve with your salad of choice.

Black Bean and Corn Salad

Total cooking and preparation time: 10 minutes

Servings: 6

Nutritional Value (Amount Per Serving)

159 Calories
49 Calories from Fat
5.6 g Total Fat
0.8 g Saturated Fat
0 mg Cholesterol
2.6 mg Sodium
23.7 g Total Carbohydrate
5.9 g Dietary Fiber
3 g Sugars
6.4 g Protein

Ingredients

- 1 can corn, drained (10 ounce)
- 1/4 cup cilantro, fresh & chopped
- 1 can black beans, drained (15 ounce)
- 1/8 cup red onion, chopped
- 1 tomatoes, chopped
- 2 tbsp. olive oil
- 3 tbsp. lemon juice
- Pepper & salt to taste

Cooking Directions

1. In a large bowl, mix together all of the ingredients & refrigerate the mixture until ready to serve.

Moroccan Chickpeas and Sweet Potatoes

Total cooking and preparation time: 40 min

Servings 4

Nutritional Value (Amount Per Serving)

311.3 Calories
41 Calories from Fat
4.6 g Total Fat
0.4 g Saturated Fat
0 mg Cholesterol
692.8 mg Sodium
60.1 g Total Carbohydrate
10.2 g Dietary Fiber
14.6 g Sugars
9.6 g Protein

Ingredients

- 2 sweet potatoes, medium, peeled & cut into pieces (preferably bite-size)
- 1 tbsp. ginger, fresh & minced
- 2 tbsp. lemon juice
- 1 tsp. paprika
- 1⁄2 tsp. red pepper flakes, crushed to taste
- 1 cup chickpea cooking liquid or water
- 1⁄4 cup apricot, dried & diced
- 2 tbsp. cooking sherry or red wine
- 1 tsp. cumin
- 1⁄4 cup raisins
- 1 tsp. cinnamon

- 2 cups chickpeas, cooked
- 1⁄4 cup almonds, sliced & toasted
- 1 onion, large & thinly sliced
- 3 garlic cloves, fresh & minced
- 1⁄2 tsp. salt

Cooking Directions

1. Mix together the onion, ginger, garlic, and sherry or wine in a medium saucepan.

2. Cover & heat approximately five minutes, over low heat settings.

3. Add the red pepper flakes, cinnamon, cumin, and paprika & cook approximately a minute longer, uncovered.

4. Add chickpea cooking liquid or water, salt, apricots and sweet potatoes and let it boil. Simmer approximately 15 minutes, until the sweet potatoes are just tender, covered.

5. Add the raisins, lemon juice, & chickpeas.

6. Cook until the chickpeas are hot, approximately five minutes, stirring occasionally.

7. Add the sliced almond

Parsley Salad

Total cooking and preparation time: 30 min

Servings: 8

Nutritional Value (Amount Per Serving)

165.2 Calories
81 Calories from Fat
9.1 g Total Fat
1.3 g Saturated Fat
0 mg Cholesterol
57.4 mg Sodium
20.1 g Total Carbohydrate
5.3 g Dietary Fiber
3.3 g Sugars
3.8 g Protein

Ingredients

- 4 tomatoes, large & finely chopped
- 1cup bulgur or burghul
- 6 onions, green & finely chopped or 6 spring onions
- Juice of 3 lemons, freshly squeeze
- 150 g flat leaf parsley, Italian parsley, fresh or parsley, fresh & finely chopped.
- 1 cup boiled water
- 1/8 tsp. each ground black pepper & salt or to taste
- 5 tbsp. olive oil

Cooking Directions

1. In a small bowl, add one cup of bulgur & one cup of boiled water and mix well. Place a tea towel at the top of the bowl and make sure that steam should remain. Kept aside at room temperature until cool.

2. Finely chop the spring onions, parsley & tomatoes and then place them into your salad bowl, large & separate.

3. Pour juice of all the fresh lemons over the salad mixture and then add olive oil, salt and black pepper in the salad mixture, mixing well.

4. Place this mixture over the cool bulgur & mix well.

5. Serve & enjoy. You may even refrigerate any leftovers for 2 to 3 days.

African Banana Coconut Bake

Total cooking and preparation time: 10 min

Servings: 8

Nutritional Value (Amount Per Serving)

189.2 Calories
53 Calories from Fat
5.9 g Total Fat
3.8 g Saturated Fat
0 mg Cholesterol
52.3 mg Sodium
35.8 g Total Carbohydrate
3.1 g Dietary Fiber
24.4 g Sugars
1.5 g Protein

Ingredients

- 3 tbsp. brown sugar, packed
- 1 tbsp. margarine, low-fat
- 2/3 cup shredded coconut
- 5 bananas, medium
- 1 tbsp. lemon juice
- 1/3 cup orange juice

Cooking Directions

1. Heat your oven to 375 F/190 C.

2. Cut the bananas into halves, crosswise & arrange in greased pie plate, preferably 9".

3. Dot with butter or margarine & drizzle lemon juices and orange.

4. Sprinkle with coconut and brown sugar.

5. Bake 8 to 10 minutes, until coconut is golden.

Kale Chips

Total cooking and preparation time: 25 min

Servings 4

Nutritional Value (Amount Per Serving)

25.1 Calories
3 Calories from Fat
0.4 g Total Fat
0 g Saturated Fat
0 mg Cholesterol
21.6 mg Sodium
5 g Total Carbohydrate
1 g Dietary Fiber
0 g Sugars
1.7 g Protein

Ingredients

- 1 bunch kale
- 1 spritz olive oil

Cooking Directions

1. Preheat your oven to 250 F/125 C. Wash the kale using cold water and then Pat dry.

2. Arrange the kale on cookie sheet; make sure pieces don't overlap each other.

3. Spray with olive oil and sprint salt over the top.

4. Cook approximately 20 minutes.

5. Remove from heat and enjoy!

Tempeh Salad

Total cooking and preparation time: 40 min

Servings 4

Nutritional Value (Amount Per Serving)

374.2 Calories
281 Calories from Fat
31.3 g Total Fat
5.2 g Saturated Fat
10.4 mg Cholesterol
511.7 mg Sodium
11.2 g Total Carbohydrate
1 g Dietary Fiber
1.4 g Sugars
16.7 g Protein

Ingredients

- 12 oz. tempeh, cubed
- 1 tbsp. parsley, fresh & chopped
- 2 tbsp. minced red bell peppers
- 1 dill pickle, large & minced
- 2 to 3 minced scallions
- 1 tsp. lemon juice
- 1/2 cup regular mayonnaise or soy mayonnaise
- 1 tbsp. yellow mustard
- Black pepper, freshly ground & salt
- 1 minced stalk celery

Cooking Directions

1. In a saucepan add salted water and bring to a boil, and then put the cubed tempeh in it.

2. Decrease the heat settings to low and simmer approximately 10 minutes, drain & set aside at room temperature to cool.

3. Combine the pepper, celery, pickle, parsley & scallion together in a large bowl.

4. To give the cubed tempeh a rough chop, run a knife all the way through and add the chopped tempeh to the bowl together with the mustard, mayonnaise, lemon, pepper & salt.

5. Fold everything as one, cover and to let the flavors combine, let it refrigerate for a minimum period of half an hour. You may even keep this in the fridge for 2 to 3 days, covered.

6. This salad goes great in a lavash wrap, on wheat toast, or in a pita pocket.

Purple Cabbage and Pecan Salad

Total cooking and preparation time: 5 min

Servings: 8

Nutritional Value (Amount Per Serving)

241 Calories
150 Calories from Fat
16.8 g Total Fat
1.8 g Saturated Fat
0 mg Cholesterol
524.5 mg Sodium
21.9 g Total Carbohydrate
4.4 g Dietary Fiber
16.9 g Sugars
3.8 g Protein

Ingredients

- 3 scallions, including the green part & chopped
- 1 cup Chinese sweetened pecans
- 1 bag coleslaw mix, or 1 head cabbage, shredded

For Dressing

- 1/4 cup oil
- 1/2 cup sugar
- 1/4 cup soy sauce
- 1/2 cup vinegar

Cooking Directions

1. Mix all the dressing ingredients separately.

2. Shake well & pour the dressing mixture over the scallions, pecans, & cabbage.

3. Mix well to evenly coat & serve immediately.

Chapter Eight: Desert

Pan Fudge Cake

Total cooking & preparation time: 30 min

Servings: 10

Nutrition Info (Estimated Amount Per Serving)

369.6 Calories
153 Calories from Fat
17 g Total Fat
2.2 g Saturated Fat
0 mg Cholesterol
365.1 mg Sodium
51.6 g Total Carbohydrate
1.5 g Dietary Fiber
30.1 g Sugars
3.4 g Protein

Ingredients

- 1 and 1/2 cups sugar
- 1/2 cup cocoa
- 1 and 1/2 tsp. baking soda
- 2 cups flour
- 3/4 tsp. salt
- 1 and 1/2 tsp. vanilla
- 3/4 cup vegetable oil
- 1 and 1/2 cups water
- 1 and 1/2 tsp. vinegar

Directions

1. Preheat your oven to 350 F/175 C.

2. Sift all of the dry ingredients together in an ungreased pan, preferably 9 x 13.

3. Add the liquids & stir for few minutes, until just blended.

4. Bake approximately half an hour.

5. Don't tear up the top of the cake as the cake would be extremely moist & frost with frosting of your choice.

Cinnamon Oranges

Total cooking & preparation time: 5 min

Servings: 2

Nutrition Info (Estimated Amount Per Serving)

71.2 Calories
0.2 g Total Fat
0 g Saturated Fat
0 mg Cholesterol
0.4 mg Sodium
18.5 g Total Carbohydrate
5.2 g Dietary Fiber
12.3 g Sugars
1.4 g Protein

Ingredients

- 1 sliced apple
- 2 oranges, sweetest
- 1 tbsp. cinnamon

Cooking Directions

1. Peel the oranges and then slice crossways into rounds & arrange the pieces on a pretty plate.

2. If desired, add a few slices of apple.

3. Dust cinnamon lightly & serve immediately.

Eggless Vegan Carrot Cake Cupcakes

Total cooking & preparation time: 40 min

Servings: 1

Nutrition Info (Estimated Amount Per Serving)

105.2 Calories
2.5 g Total Fat
0.2 g Saturated Fat
0 mg Cholesterol
183.9 mg Sodium
19.6 g Total Carbohydrate
0.9 g Dietary Fiber
8.8 g Sugars
1.5 g Protein

Ingredients

- 2 and 1/2 cups flour
- 1/2 tsp. nutmeg
- 1 and 1/2 tsp. baking powder
- 3/4 cup sugar
- 1/2 cup applesauce, unsweetened
- 1 and 1/2 tsp. cinnamon
- 2 cups grated carrots
- 1 cup pineapple, crushed
- 2 tsp. baking soda
- 1/4 cup canola oil
- 1/2 tsp. salt

Cooking Directions

1. Mix baking powder and apple sauce in a small bowl, make a foamy mixture and keep it aside.

2. Mix cinnamon, sugar, flour, baking soda, salt, and nutmeg in a large bowl.

3. Add carrots, oil, applesauce mixture & pineapple, mixing well.

4. If desired, add nuts, raisins or coconut, flaked.

5. Scoop the mixture into cupcake liners, approximately 24.

6. Bake at 160 C/ 325 F until toothpick comes out clean, when inserted or approximately half an hour.

7. Set it aside at room temperature, once cooled, frost with icing (water, 'fake' butter, powdered sugar and vanilla).

Scrum-Diddly-Umptious Vegan Brownies

Total cooking & preparation time: 40 min

Servings: 9

Nutrition Info (Estimated Amount Per Serving)

101.4 Calories
0.6 g Total Fat
0.3 g Saturated Fat
0 mg Cholesterol
281.4 mg Sodium
24.3 g Total Carbohydrate
1.6 g Dietary Fiber
13.8 g Sugars
1.8 g Protein

Ingredients

* 1/2 cup vegan chocolate chips, semisweet
* 3/4 cup white flour, unbleached
* 1 cup applesauce, unsweetened
* 1/3 cup cocoa powder
* 1 tsp. vanilla
* 1/2 cup raw sugar
* 2 tsp. baking powder
* 1/3 cup walnuts
* 1/2 tsp. baking soda
* 1 dash cinnamon
* 1/2 tsp. salt

Cooking Directions

1. Preheat your oven to 350 F/ 175 C and lightly oil or spray a baking pan, preferably 8 x 8.

2. In a medium bowl, mix together the sugar, applesauce, & vanilla. Whisk together the cocoa, flour, baking soda, baking powder, cinnamon and salt in a separate bowl.

3. In the middle of the dry ingredients, make a well & add the applesauce mixture. Mix until just combined and then fold gently in the chocolate chips & walnuts.

4. Spread in the prepared pan & bake until center is firm & not sticky, approximately half an hour.

5. Before slicing, let it cool completely.

Silky Chocolate Peanut Butter Pie

Total cooking and preparation time: 10 min

Servings: 8

Nutrition Info (Estimated Amount Per Serving)

455.2 Calories
26.1 g Total Fat
7.7 g Saturated Fat
0 mg Cholesterol
274.6 mg Sodium
51.3 g Total Carbohydrate
3 g Dietary Fiber
38.1 g Sugars
10.3 g Protein

Ingredients

- 16 oz. silken tofu, soft & drained
- 1 cup chocolate chips
- 2/3 cup creamy peanut butter
- 1 graham cracker crust, prepared
- 1/2 tsp. vanilla
- 1/2 cup sugar

Cooking Directions

1. Over high heat settings in a microwave, melt the chocolate chips in a small bowl approximately 90 seconds. Stir until smooth. Allow it to cool slightly at the room temperature.

2. Place peanut butter, tofu, vanilla & sugar either in a food processor or blender & whirl until smooth.

3. Add chocolate & whirl until just combined.

4. Pour into the crust.

5. Cover with plastic wrap & refrigerate until filling is set, for several hours.

6. Garnish with melted chocolate, whipped cream or peanuts.

Zucchini Brownies

Total cooking and preparation time: 45 min

Servings: 24

Nutrition Info (Estimated Amount Per Serving)

138 Calories
4.8 g Total Fat
0.6 g Saturated Fat
0 mg Cholesterol
150.6 mg Sodium
21.9 g Total Carbohydrate
0.7 g Dietary Fiber
12.9 g Sugars
1.5 g Protein

Ingredients

- 2 cups flour
- 1 and 1/2 cups sugar
- 1 tsp. salt
- 1 tsp. baking soda
- 1/2 cup cocoa
- 2 tbsp. vanilla
- 1/2 cup oil
- 2 cups zucchini, peeled & grated

Cooking Directions

1. In a large bowl, mix together the cocoa, flour, salt, sugar, & baking soda.

2. Add the zucchini, oil, and vanilla; mixing well.

3. Bake in an ungreased pan at 350 F/175 C approximately half a minute, preferably 9 x 13".

Fruit Salad

Total cooking & preparation time: 15 min

Servings: 4

Nutrition Info (Estimated Amount Per Serving)

275.7 Calories
14.2 g Total Fat
12.3 g Saturated Fat
0 mg Cholesterol
10.6 mg Sodium
39.7 g Total Carbohydrate
7.4 g Dietary Fiber
27.5 g 110 Sugars
3.1 g Protein

Ingredients

- 1 cup ripe mango, diced & peeled
- 1 tbsp. fresh lime, zest & juice
- 1 cup orange section
- 1 cup banana, sliced
- 1/8 tsp. each ground cinnamon, cardamom & ginger
- 1 tbsp. sugar, dark brown
- 2 cups cubed pineapple, fresh

Garnish

- 1 cup coconut, toasted

Cooking Directions

1. In a bowl, preferably medium sized, mix the salad ingredients together, gently toss to combine. Cover & let it chill approximately an hour.

2. Sprinkle toasted coconut over the dessert.

Peanut Butter/Corn Flakes Cookies

Total cooking and preparation time: 15 min

Servings: 24 to 36 cookies

Nutrition Info (Estimated Amount Per Serving)

160.9 Calories
5.5 g Total Fat
1.1 g Saturated Fat
0 mg Cholesterol
108.8 mg Sodium
27.4 g Total Carbohydrate
0.8 g Dietary Fiber
13.8 g Sugars
3.2 g Protein

Ingredients

- 6 to 7 cups corn flakes
- 1 cup peanut butter (crunchy or smooth)
- 1 cup white corn syrup
- 1 cup sugar

Cooking Directions

1. Bring corn syrup and sugar to boil and then remove from the heat.

2. Put the peanut butter in; mixing well.

3. Transfer the mixture over the corn flakes.

4. Spread into buttered pan or mix into balls onto waxed paper.

Chocolate Cake

Total cooking & Preparation time: 5 min

Servings: 1

Nutrition Info (Estimated Amount Per Serving)

377.3 Calories
7.5 g Total Fat
1.2 g Saturated Fat
0 mg Cholesterol
609.1 mg Sodium
75.6 g Total Carbohydrate
1.7 g Dietary Fiber
50.2 g Sugars
3.8 g Protein

Ingredients

- 1⁄4 cup flour
- 1⁄2 tbsp. cocoa powder, unsweetened
- 1⁄4 cup sugar
- 3⁄4 tsp. white vinegar
- 1⁄4 tsp. baking soda
- 1⁄2 tbsp. vegetable oil
- 1⁄4 cup water
- 1⁄4 tsp. vanilla
- 1⁄8 tsp. salt

Cooking Directions

1. In a large coffee cup, stir all of the dry ingredients together.

2. Add the wet ingredients and use a fork to mix the ingredients well.

3. Microwave on half power on the rotating plate approximately three minutes.

Vegan Peanut Butter Chocolate Chip Oatmeal Cookies

Total cooking & preparation time: 20 min

Servings: 36

Nutrition Info (Estimated Amount Per Serving)

167.1 Calories
6.7 g Total Fat
1.8 g Saturated Fat
0 mg Cholesterol
133.9 mg Sodium
25.6 g Total Carbohydrate
1.8 g Dietary Fiber
16 g Sugars
3.2 g Protein

Ingredients

- 1 and 1/3 cups chocolate chips, semi-sweet
- 4 tbsp. vegetable oil
- 2 cups sugar, light brown
- 1 tsp. baking soda
- 2 tsp. pure vanilla extract
- 1 cup flour, whole wheat
- 2/3 cup soymilk
- 1 cup flour, all-purpose
- 2 cups rolled oats
- 2/3 cup + 2 tbsp. peanut butter, crunchy
- 1 tsp. salt

Cooking Directions

1. Preheat your oven to 190 C/375 F.

2. Stir together the peanut butter, vegetable oil, light brown sugar & soymilk in a large mixing bowl.

3. Thoroughly stir the soda, salt & flour together in a small bowl.

4. Stir into batter.

5. Stir in chocolate chips and oats.

6. By rounded tablespoonful, drop the batter onto parchment lined baking sheet or Silpat.

7. Bake until set, approximately 10 minutes.

8. Remove the sheet from the oven & let it cool on a tray approximately 5 minutes at room temperature.

Vegan Banana Oat Cookies

Total cooking & preparation time: 33 minutes

Servings 36

Nutrition Info (Estimated Amount Per Serving)

113.3 Calories
2.9 g Total Fat
0.4 g Saturated Fat
0 mg Cholesterol
70 mg Sodium
20 g Total Carbohydrate
1.3 g Dietary Fiber
9.1 g Sugars
2.2 g Protein

Ingredients

- 2 and 1/4 cups oats
- 1 banana, mashed
- 1 and 1/2 tsp. vanilla extract
- 1/3 cup + 1 tsp. oil, plus
- 1 cup brown sugar
- 1 and 1/2 cups flour
- 1/2 cup sugar
- 1 tsp. baking soda
- 1 and 1/2 tsp. cinnamon
- 1/2 tsp. salt

Cooking Directions

1. Mix together the baking soda, flour, salt, and cinnamon and keep it aside.

2. Mix together the sugar, brown sugar, water, and oil in a separate bowl.

3. Add the vanilla & banana.

4. Stir in the flour mixture; mixing well.

5. Stir in the oats.

6. Let the mixture sit for a minute, if it seems too thin, so the excess liquid can be absorbed by the oats.

7. Preheat your oven to 175 C/350 F.

8. By tablespoonful, drop the cookies onto a cookie sheet, greased.

9. Cook until done, approximately 15 minutes.

Vegan Chocolate Chip Cookies

Total cooking & preparation time: 30 min

Servings: 36

Nutrition Info (Estimated Amount Per Serving)

116.9 Calories
4.7 g Total Fat
1.8 g Saturated Fat
0 mg Cholesterol
130.4 mg Sodium
18.5 g Total Carbohydrate
0.6 g Dietary Fiber
11.1 g Sugars
1.2 g Protein

Ingredients

- 1 and 1⁄2 cups chocolate chips, semi-sweet or vegan carob chips
- 2 tsp. vanilla extract
- 1 and 1⁄4 cups sugar
- 1 tbsp. molasses
- 1 tsp. baking soda
- 2 and 1⁄2 cups flour, all-purpose
- 1 cup margarine
- 1 tsp. salt

Cooking Directions

1. Preheat your oven to 175 C/350 F.

2. Using a hand mixer, cream the sugar and margarine until fluffy. Add the vanilla and molasses and incorporate. Add all of the dry ingredients to the mixture & mix until a dough forms, for few minutes. Fold chocolate chips into the dough.

3. Drop the dough by tablespoons or roll the dough into balls, preferably 1" onto cookie sheets, ungreased. Bake until mildly browned, approximately 8 to 10 minutes. Let the cookies to cool at room temperature approximately 5 minutes, on the baking sheets. Then transfer the cookies to the cooling racks, cool & enjoy!

Thai Coconut-Mango Sticky Rice

Total cooking & preparation time: 35 min

Servings 3

Nutrition Info (Estimated Amount Per Serving)

570.9 Calories
29.6 g Total Fat
25.3 g Saturated Fat
0 mg Cholesterol
20.8 mg Sodium
77.6 g Total Carbohydrate
2.9 g Dietary Fiber
48.8 g Sugars
6 g Protein

Ingredients

- 1⁄2 cup sweet Asian rice or jasmine rice or basmati rice
- 1 can coconut milk, (14 oz.)
- 1⁄2 cup sugar
- 1 mango, sliced

Cooking Directions

1. Cook rice as per the directions mentioned on the package, add half the sugar. (You need to substitute the coconut milk for half of the water).

2. When you are done with the rice, it should not have any liquid and should be fairly dry in the pot.

3. Boil the remaining coconut milk with the remaining sugar in a saucepan, preferably medium sized.

4. Let it boil at high heat settings until it reaches a thick, syrupy consistency, few minutes.

5. Arrange the cooked coconut rice in a plate or bowl with the mango slices and drip a small quantity of sauce over the complete thing.

Healthy Banana Oatmeal Sponge Cookies

Total cooking & preparation time: 25 min

Servings: 12

Nutrition Info (Estimated Amount Per Serving)

79.1 Calories
8 Calories from Fat
1 g Total Fat
0.2 g Saturated Fat
0 mg Cholesterol
2.9 mg Sodium
16.4 g Total Carbohydrate
2 g Dietary Fiber
4.1 g Sugars
2 g Protein

Ingredients

- 2 cups oatmeal
- 1 cup ripe banana, mashed
- 1/2 tsp. vanilla
- 1/4 cup applesauce
- 1/2 tsp. cinnamon
- 1/3 cup raisins

Cooking Directions

1. Heat your oven to 350 F/175 C.

2. Mix everything together until moist, gooey and sticky, for few minutes.

3. Drop by tablespoonful onto the baking sheet, ungreased.

4. Flatten to your desired thickness & shape on the baking sheet.

5. Bake at 175C/350 F approximately 15 minutes.

6. Remove the cookies and let it cool at wire rack.

Lemon Gem Cupcakes

Total cooking & preparation time: 35 min

Servings: 12

Nutrition Info (Estimated Amount Per Serving)

225.4 Calories
4.8 g Total Fat
0.4 g Saturated Fat
0 mg Cholesterol
145.8 mg Sodium
44.8 g Total Carbohydrate
0.5 g Dietary Fiber
33.2 g Sugars
1.6 g Protein

Ingredients

- 3/4 tsp. baking soda
- 1 and 1/3 cups all-purpose flour
- 1/2 tsp. baking powder
- 1 tbsp. lemon zest
- 2/3 cup plus 2 tbsp. sugar
- 1/4 cup lemon juice
- 1 tsp. vanilla extract
- 1/4 cup canola oil
- 1 cup rice milk
- 1/4 tsp. salt

Frosting

- 2 cups confectioners' sugar, sifted
- 1⁄4 cup soymilk
- 2 tbsp. lemon juice
- 1⁄4 cup vegan margarine, non hydrogenated & softened

Cooking Directions

1. Preheat your oven to 350 F/175 C.

2. Line a muffin tin, preferably with 12 slots with paper liners.

3. Sift together the baking soda, baking powder, flour & salt.

4. Combine vanilla, oil, rice milk, sugar, lemon zest and juice in a separate bowl.

5. Mix the dry mixture with the wet mixture until smooth, mixing well.

6. Fill every muffin tin approximately 2/3 full and bake the cupcakes approximately 15 to 20 minutes.

7. Remove the cupcakes from muffin tin and then place them on a wire cooling rack.

8. When fully cooled, frost them.

9. In the meantime, using a hand mixer beat the margarine until fluffy.

10. Stir in lemon juice & soy milk.

11. Add confectioners' sugar & mix until smooth. Frost the cupcakes.

Vegan Cream Cheese Frosting

Total cooking & preparation time: 10 min

Servings: 12

Nutrition Info (Estimated Amount Per Serving)

78.8 Calories
0 g Saturated Fat
0 mg Cholesterol
0.4 mg Sodium
20 g Total Carbohydrate
0 g Dietary Fiber
19.6 g Sugars
0 g Protein

Ingredients

- 1 tsp. vanilla extract
- 1/4 cup vegan cream cheese, softened, Tofutti
- 2 cups confectioners' sugar, sifted
- 1/4 cup margarine, non-hydrogenated & softened

Cooking Directions

1. Cream the cream cheese & margarine together until just combined.

2. Whip while adding the confectioners' sugar in 1/2 cup batches, using a handheld mixer. Mix until creamy and smooth, then mix in the vanilla. Keep covered & refrigerate until ready to use.

Chocolate Vegan Brownies

Total cooking & preparation time: 55 min

Servings: 12

Nutrition Info (Estimated Amount Per Serving)

120.8 Calories
3.2 g Total Fat
1.6 g Saturated Fat
0 mg Cholesterol
391.9 mg Sodium
22.3 g Total Carbohydrate
2.2 g Dietary Fiber
6.9 g Sugars
3.3 g Protein

Ingredients

- 1/2 cup ghiradelli cocoa powder, unsweetened
- 3/4 tsp. baking powder
- 1 and 1/2 cups white flour, unbleached
- 1/3 cup applesauce, unsweetened (gravenstein)
- 1 and 1/2 tsp. baking soda
- 1/2 cup chocolate chips, semi-sweet
- 1 and 1/2 cups soymilk, chocolate
- 1 and 1/2 cups turbinado sugar
- 1 tsp. sea salt

Cooking Directions

1. Lightly oil a glass pan, preferably 9 x 12 with vegetable oil.

2. Preheat your oven to 325 F/160 C.

3. Mix together the cocoa, flour, baking powder, sugar, sea salt & baking soda using a fork.

4. Blend the applesauce & chocolate soy milk in a small bowl.

5. Thoroughly mix together the wet ingredients with the dry ingredients.

6. Fold this mixture in the chocolate chips and pour the batter into an oiled pan. Bake approximately half an hour or little more (remember that smaller pans may have a longer cooking time).

Candied Pecans

Total cooking & preparation time: 5 min

Servings: 1/2 cup

Nutrition Info (Estimated Amount Per Serving)

893.8 Calories
641 Calories from Fat
71.2 g Total Fat
6.1 g Saturated Fat
0 mg Cholesterol
16.3 mg Sodium
67.9 g Total Carbohydrate
9.5 g Dietary Fiber
57.5 g Sugars
9.1 g Protein

Ingredients

- 2 tbsp. brown sugar
- 1/2 cup pecan halves
- 1 tbsp. water

Cooking Directions

1. Preheat your oven to 375 F/190 C.

2. First toss the pecans with water and then with the brown sugar.

3. Place the nuts on a parchment-lined baking sheet and bake until sugar is caramelized, approximately five to ten minutes.

4. Slide the parchment with nuts off and let the pan to cool a bit; set aside.

Peanut Butter Krispies Treats

Total cooking & preparation time: 12 min

Servings: 12 squares

Nutrition Info (Estimated Amount Per Serving)

317.7 Calories
11 g Total Fat
2.3 g Saturated Fat
0 mg Cholesterol
232.2 mg Sodium
52.5 g Total Carbohydrate
1.4 g Dietary Fiber
26.7 g Sugars
6.3 g Protein

Ingredients

- 6 cups Rice Krispies
- 1 cup corn syrup
- 1 cup peanut butter, smooth
- 1 cup sugar

Cooking Directions

1. Grease a baking pan, preferably 13 x 9".

2. Over low heat settings in large saucepan stir the corn syrup, sugar & peanut butter together.

3. Let it boil approximately three minutes, stirring constantly.

4. Remove the pan from the heat.

5. Add cereal, toss & coat with the cooked mixture until evenly coated.

6. Press speedily into the pan.

7. Let it cool at the room temperature and then cut into squares.

Vegan Brownie-Oat Cookies

Total cooking & preparation time: 15 min

Servings 20

Nutrition Info (Estimated Amount Per Serving)

78 Calories
0.9 g Total Fat
0.3 g Saturated Fat
0 mg Cholesterol
19.4 mg Sodium
16.5 g Total Carbohydrate
1.6 g Dietary Fiber
6.6 g Sugars
2.2 g Protein

Ingredients

- 1 cup oats
- 2/3 cup flour
- 1 egg substitute
- 1/2 cup cocoa powder
- 1/3 cup maple syrup
- 1 tsp. baking powder
- 1/3 cup sugar
- 1 tsp. vanilla

Cooking Directions

1. Mix the vanilla, egg replacer & syrup together.

2. Add this mixture to the dry ingredients & stir until moistened, for few minutes.

3. Make small balls & bake on cookie sheets, greased at 175 C/ 350 F approximately 10 minutes.

Cranberry Whip

Total cooking & preparation time: 20 min

Servings: 4

Nutrition Info (Estimated Amount Per Serving)

270.6 Calories
0.1 g Total Fat
0 g Saturated Fat
0 mg Cholesterol
45.1 mg Sodium
67.5 g Total Carbohydrate
2.6 g Dietary Fiber
1.9 g Sugars
1.8 g Protein

Ingredients

- 2 cups cranberries, fresh
- 1 and 1⁄2 cups water
- 1 cup sugar, granulated
- 1 cup water
- 1 dash salt
- 1⁄3 cup farina

Cooking Directions

1. Heat the cranberries in 1 and 1/2 cups of water, bring to a boil and then decrease the heat settings. Simmer until berries pop, uncovered, approximately 8 to 10 minutes.

2. To remove the skins, press the cranberries using a sieve. Return the juice to the saucepan. Add 1 cup water, salt and sugar; bring to a boil again.

3. Gradually add the farina, stirring constantly. Cook 3 to 5 minutes, until thickened, stirring occasionally.

4. Put the mixture into a mixer bowl, preferably small. Beat on high speed approximately 3 to 5 minutes, until pudding becomes light pink and fluffy.

Apple Dessert

Total cooking & preparation time: 15minutes

Servings: 1

Nutrition Info (Estimated Amount Per Serving)

393 Calories
0.6 g Total Fat
0.1 g Saturated Fat
0 mg Cholesterol
6.1 mg Sodium
102.8 g Total Carbohydrate
7.9 g Dietary Fiber
90.1 g Sugars
0.9 g Protein

Ingredients

- 3 cups apples, peeled & sliced (Golden Delicious, Fuji, or Rome)
- 1 tbsp. maple syrup
- 1 dash cinnamon
- 3 and 1/2 tbsp. sugar

Cooking Directions

1. Peel & slice the apples and then put the slices in a microwave safe bowl.

2. Sprinkle with cinnamon & sugar.

3. Microwave approximately five minutes, check apples frequently for desired doneness. Give them half a minute more until done, if not done.

4. To cover the apples with the sugar mixture, stir the apples with cinnamon/sugar, after removing.

5. Add ice cream and maple syrup.

Chocolate Frosting

Total cooking & preparation time: 10 minutes

Servings: 12

Nutrition Info (Estimated Amount Per Serving)

107 Calories
2.4 g Total Fat
0.3 g Saturated Fat
0 mg Cholesterol
98 mg Sodium
21.3 g Total Carbohydrate
0.4 g Dietary Fiber
16.7 g Sugars
0.3 g Protein

Ingredients

- 6 tbsp. cornstarch
- 1 cup sugar
- 1/2 tsp. vanilla
- 4 tbsp. cocoa
- 1 cup water
- 1/2 tsp. salt
- 2 tbsp. oil

Cooking Directions

1. In a medium sauce pan, mix together the cornstarch, sugar, cocoa, and salt.

2. Whisk in the water.

3. Over medium high heat settings, heat until starts boiling & gets thick. Boil approximately a minute or two.

4. Remove the pan from the heat & stir in vanilla & oil. Cool & spread on cake, cooled.

Baked Apple Slices

Total cooking & preparation time: 20 minutes

Servings: 6

Nutrition Info (Estimated Amount Per Serving)

539 Calories
1.8 g Total Fat
0.2 g Saturated Fat
0 mg Cholesterol
3.1 mg Sodium
137 g Total Carbohydrate
7.8 g Dietary Fiber
124.6 g Sugars
1.3 g Protein

Ingredients

- 1 and 1/2 tsp. cinnamon
- 1/3 cup flour, all-purpose
- 4 apples
- 1/3 cup sugar, granulated

Cooking Directions

1. Peel, halve & core the apples. Cut each apple half into wedges, preferably six.

2. Mix together the cinnamon, sugar & flour in a large bowl, mixing well.

3. Add the apples & toss well.

4. Spread apples on parchment paper-lined or non-stick baking sheet in a single layer.

5. Bake in pre-heated oven 230 C /450 F until tender & browned, approximately 15 to 20 minutes.

6. Before removing from the baking sheet, let it cool at the room temperature for a few minutes.

7. Serve warm.

Pumpkin Brownie Muffins

Total cooking & preparation time: 10 minutes

Servings: 12

Nutrition Info (Estimated Amount Per Serving)

191.6 Calories
6.7 g Total Fat
1.4 g Saturated Fat
0 mg Cholesterol
351.8 mg Sodium
33.4 g Total Carbohydrate
1.2 g Dietary Fiber
16.8 g Sugars
2.9 g Protein

Ingredients

- 1 can solid pack pumpkin, (15 oz.)
- 1 box devil's food cake mix, (18 oz.)

Cooking Directions

1. Mix both the ingredients together. Make sure you don't add anything else to the mixture.

2. Place the batter into mini muffin tins (or muffin tins) sprayed with non-stick spray, or lined with paper.

3. Make 36 mini muffins or 12 regular and bake at 400 F/200 C approximately 20 minutes..

Blueberry Sauce / Topping

Total cooking & preparation time: 10 min

Servings 8

Nutrition Info (Estimated Amount Per Serving)

50.3 Calories
0.1 g Total Fat
0 g Saturated Fat
0 mg Cholesterol
0.5 mg Sodium
13 g Total Carbohydrate
0.9 g Dietary Fiber
10 g Sugars
0.3 g Protein

Ingredients

- Juice and zest of 1 lemon
- 1/8 tsp. cardamom
- 2 cups blueberries, fresh & washed
- 1/4 cup sugar
- 1/8 tsp. cinnamon
- 1 tbsp. cornstarch
- 1/4 cup orange juice or Grand Marnier

Directions

1. In a small pot, put everything together but don't add the Grand Marnier, stir to blend. Cook until thick, approximately four to five minutes. Add the Marnier stir & let it cool.

Quick Elephant Ears

Total cooking & preparation time: 10 minutes

Servings 10

Nutrition Info (Estimated Amount Per Serving)

210.9 Calories
2.3 g Total Fat
0.6 g Saturated Fat
0 mg Cholesterol
190.9 mg Sodium
45.8 g Total Carbohydrate
1.2 g Dietary Fiber
30.6 g Sugars
2.5 g Protein

Ingredients

- 10 flour tortillas (approximately 7")
- 2 tsp. cinnamon, ground
- 1 and 1⁄2 cups sugar
- oil (for frying)

Cooking Directions

2. In a large plate or shallow bowl, mix the cinnamon and sugar together; keep it aside.

3. Heat 1/2" of oil in a skillet.

4. Place the tortilla in the skillet, one at a time.

5. Cook approximately 5 seconds; turn & cook until browned, approximately 10 more seconds.

6. Place in the sugar mixture, turning to coat.

7. Serve immediately.

Crazy Cake

Total cooking & preparation time: 45 min

Servings: 12

Nutrition Info (Estimated Amount Per Serving)

376.9 Calories
127 Calories from Fat
14.1 g Total Fat
1.9 g Saturated Fat
0 mg Cholesterol
406 mg Sodium
59.2 g Total Carbohydrate
1.5 g Dietary Fiber
33.4 g Sugars
3.9 g Protein

Ingredients

- 2 cups sugar
- 3 cups flour
- 2 tbsp. unflavored vinegar
- 1/2 cup cocoa
- 2 tsp. baking soda
- 2 cups water
- 1 tsp. vanilla
- 3/4 cup salad oil
- 1 tsp. salt

Cooking Directions

1. In a large bowl, mix all of the dry ingredients together, removing any lumps from the mixture.

2. Add the liquids & mix for few seconds, until smooth.

3. Pour the mixture into an ungreased pan, preferably 9x14 and bake at 350 F/ 175 C approximately half an hour or little more.

Chapter Nine: Smoothies

Chocolate Smoothy

Total cooking & preparation time: 5 min

Total Servings: 2

Nutritional Value (Amount Per Serving)

341.4 Calories
37 Calories from Fat
4.2 g Total Fat
0.8 g Saturated Fat
0 mg Cholesterol
95 mg Sodium
79.7 g Total Carbohydrate
12.4 g Dietary Fiber
58.6 g Sugars
8.2 g Protein

Ingredients

- 2 cups blueberries, frozen
- 1 tbsp. ground flax seeds
- 5 oz. Baby Spinach, organic
- 1/2 cup almond or soymilk
- 2 medjool dates
- 1 banana, medium
- 2 tbsp. cocoa powder

Cooking Directions

1. Put all the ingredients either in a high speed blender or a food processer and process until smooth. Enjoy!

Green Mango Smoothie

Total cooking & preparation time: 5 min

Total Servings: 1

Nutritional Value (Amount Per Serving)

417 Calories
25 Calories from Fat
2.8 g Total Fat
0.7 g Saturated Fat
0 mg Cholesterol
61.2 mg Sodium
102.8 g Total Carbohydrate
12.1 g Dietary Fiber
92 g Sugars
7.2 g Protein

Ingredients

- 2 mangoes, ripe, peeled & diced
- 2 cups spinach
- 1 to 2 cup coconut water or normal water

Cooking Directions

1. Put all the ingredients either in a high speed blender or a food processer and process until smooth (Adding the coconut water or normal water according to your desired consistency).

Favorite Smoothie

Total cooking & preparation time: 10 min

Total Servings: 2

Nutritional Value (Amount Per Serving)

357.8 Calories
178 Calories from Fat
19.8 g Total Fat
2.3 g Saturated Fat
0 mg Cholesterol
112.4 mg Sodium
44.4 g Total Carbohydrate
9.3 g Dietary Fiber
24.3 g Sugars
8 g Protein

Ingredients

- 1⁄4 cup orange juice
- 1⁄2 cup nondairy soymilk
- 1 banana, frozen
- 2 tsp. flax seeds, freshly ground
- 1⁄2 avocado
- 1⁄3 cup strawberries, frozen
- 1⁄2 cup blueberries, frozen
- 2 tbsp. almond butter

Cooking Directions

1. Put all the ingredients either in a high speed blender or a food processer and process until smooth (Adding the frozen or liquid ingredients as per your requirement to thicken or thin your smoothie). Enjoy!

Coffee Slushie

Total cooking & preparation time: 5 min

Total Servings: 2

Nutritional Value (Amount Per Serving)

68.4 Calories
19 Calories from Fat
2.2 g Total Fat
0.3 g Saturated Fat
0 mg Cholesterol
70.3 mg Sodium
8 g Total Carbohydrate
0.8 g Dietary Fiber
5 g Sugars
4.1 g Protein

Ingredients

- 250 ml soymilk, coffee-flavor
- 1/2 tsp. vanilla extract or 1/8 tsp. vanilla bean seeds
- 18 frozen coffee ice cubes

Cooking Directions

1. Using any other heavy instrument or a rolling pin, crush the ice cubes in a freezer bag or in your blender.

2. Put all the ingredients either in a high speed blender or a food processer and process until smooth. Enjoy!

Kiwi Slushi

Total cooking & preparation time: 5 Min

Total Servings: 2

Nutritional Value (Amount Per Serving)

42.1 Calories
3 Calories from Fat
0.4 g Total Fat
0 g Saturated Fat
0 mg Cholesterol
7.8 mg Sodium
10.1 g Total Carbohydrate
2.1 g Dietary Fiber
6.2 g Sugars
0.8 g Protein

Ingredients

- 2 medium ripe kiwi fruits, sliced & frozen
- 1 cup vanilla rice milk (250 ml)
- 18 chocolate tea ice cubes

Cooking Directions

1. Using any other heavy instrument or a rolling pin, crush the ice cubes in a freezer bag or in your blender.

2. Put all the ingredients either in a high speed blender or a food processer and process until smooth. Enjoy!

Enzyme Smoothie

Total cooking & preparation time: 5 Min

Total Servings: 1

Nutritional Value (Amount Per Serving)

234 Calories
6 Calories from Fat
0.8 g Total Fat
0.2 g Saturated Fat
0 mg Cholesterol
6.9 mg Sodium
60.3 g Total Carbohydrate
7.8 g Dietary Fiber
37 g Sugars
3 g Protein

Ingredients

- 1 cup fresh & ripe pineapple, chopped
- 1 cup fresh & ripe papaya, chopped
- 1 banana, frozen

Cooking Directions

1. Put all the ingredients either in a high speed blender or a food processer (add as much water as needed to reach your desired smoothie consistency) and process until smooth. Drink up!

Berry Smoothie

Total cooking & preparation time: 10 Min

Total Servings: 2

Nutritional Value (Amount Per Serving)

135.7 Calories
5 Calories from Fat
0.6 g Total Fat
0.1 g Saturated Fat
0 mg Cholesterol
2.4 mg Sodium
33.2 g Total Carbohydrate
3.2 g Dietary Fiber
22.5 g Sugars
1.9 g Protein

Ingredients

- 10 blueberries
- 1 cup freshly squeezed orange juice or grapefruit juice
- 6 strawberries, hulled & washed well
- 1 banana, large & peeled
- 4 blackberries
- 1 dates, fresh
- 4 raspberries

Cooking Directions

1. Put all the ingredients either in a high speed blender or a food processer and process until smooth. Enjoy!

Coconut-Citrus Julius

Total cooking & preparation time: 10 Min

Total Servings: 2

Nutritional Value (Amount Per Serving)

590.1 Calories
318 Calories from Fat
35.4 g Total Fat
29.4 g Saturated Fat
0 mg Cholesterol
163.1 mg Sodium
62.8 g Total Carbohydrate
6.5 g Dietary Fiber
52 g Sugars
13 g Protein

Ingredients

- 6 ice cubes
- 1 cup vanilla-flavored soymilk or plain soymilk
- 1 tbsp. lemon juice, fresh
- 1 and 1/4 cups coconut milk
- 1 tbsp. agave syrup
- 6 oz. orange juice concentrate, frozen

Cooking Directions

1. Put all the ingredients either in a high speed blender or a food processer and process until smooth (add six ice cubes at one time and taste to adjust the sweetness). Enjoy!

Coconut Peach Smoothie

Total cooking & preparation time: 5 Min

Total Servings: 4

Nutritional Value (Amount Per Serving)

155 Calories
40 Calories from Fat
4.4 g Total Fat
2.5 g Saturated Fat
15.8 mg Cholesterol
30.2 mg Sodium
27.5 g Total Carbohydrate
3.2 g Dietary Fiber
24.4 g Sugars
3 g Protein

Ingredients

- 1 cup vanilla ice cream
- 5 sliced & seeded peaches, large & fresh
- 1 can organic light coconut milk (14 oz.)
- 2 tsp. pure vanilla extract
- 1 tbsp. agave nectar
- 1 cup filtered water

Cooking Directions

1. Wash & slice the peaches; removing the pits from the peaches.

2. Put all the ingredients either in a high speed blender or a food processer and process until smooth. Enjoy!

Almond Milk

Total cooking & preparation time: 5 Min

Total Servings: 3

Nutritional Value (Amount Per Serving)

293 Calories
215 Calories from Fat
24 g Total Fat
1.9 g Saturated Fat
0 mg Cholesterol
165.5 mg Sodium
14.7 g Total Carbohydrate
5 g Dietary Fiber
6 g Sugars
9.7 g Protein

Ingredients

- 1 tbsp. date molasses
- 3 cups spring water
- 1 cup almonds

Cooking Directions

1. Put all the ingredients either in a high speed blender or a food processer and process until smooth.

2. Using a cheese cloth, strain the mixture & remove the remaining solids.

3. Refrigerate until ready to use.

Brown Rice Banana Smoothie

Total cooking & preparation time: 5 Min

Total Servings: 2

Nutritional Value (Amount Per Serving)

174.9 Calories
3 Calories from Fat
0.4 g Total Fat
0.1 g Saturated Fat
0 mg Cholesterol
292.9 mg Sodium
44.5 g Total Carbohydrate
3.1 g Dietary Fiber
31.9 g Sugars
1.4 g Protein

Ingredients

- 2 tbsp. raw honey
- 1 tsp. natural vanilla extract
- 2 organic bananas, frozen & really ripe
- 1 pinch of Celtic sea salt
- 2 cups brown rice milk, homemade

Cooking Directions

1. Put all the ingredients either in a high speed blender or a food processer and process until smooth. Enjoy!

Conclusion/Bonus

Thank you for downloading this book!

I hope this book have provided you with the necessary knowledge to better your Vegan lifestyle.

Finally, if you enjoyed this book, then I'd like to ask you for a favor, would you be kind enough to leave a review for this book on Amazon? It'd be greatly appreciated! Even if you think this book can use some improvements please let me know and I will take action upon it.

Type in the URL below to leave a review for this book on Amazon!

http://amzn.to/1PoKELY

Thank you and Happy Eating

But Wait There is More!

In order to show my sincere gratitude for you to choose my book to help you on your Vegan Journey I am giving you a Free book.

By going to the link below you can download another book for FREE

http://bit.ly/1PoKUe4

Made in the USA
Lexington, KY
08 September 2016